LOVING

by

~WILL~

Jane — with love
Tim

HIS 154
SUNBURSTS NOW
AT LAST IN PLAIN
INGLISH !

Timothy Adès

Loving by Will

William Shakespeare's Sonnets translated by Timothy Adès

First Edition 30th November 2016
ISBN: 978-1-907435-35-5

Published by Dempsey & Windle

15 Rosetrees
Guildford
Surrey
GU1 2HS
01483 571164
dempseyandwindle.co.uk

Two sonnets from the present book appeared in
Acumen Literary Journal.
Twenty-four appeared in Long Poem Magazine.
Thanks are due to the editors of these publications.

Printed by ImprintDigital, Upton Pyne, Exeter EX5 5HY UK

Introduction

This is a book of lipograms. You'll find in it all our usual consonants, plus A, I, O, and U.

What's so good about that? Words clang and bang; rhyming shifts its status from long shot to odds-on probability. Lucidity gains ground, obscurity is thrown away. And it's a lot of fun!

Why put Will of Stratford through this? Is it right for our national bard, indisputably an immortal, an Olympian, a world champion?

It is totally right. Most of us know only a tiny proportion of this moving and dramatic book of his amorous avowals, his ups and downs, his ducking and dodging as Cupid's darts crowd in. Whilst his virtuosity must win our admiration, his idiom is far from limpid. Try as you may, you just cannot follow his thoughts, cannot catch his drift. This book is a simplification, you might in fact say a translation, which you cannot afford to do without.

Buon viaggio!

To Mr W. H.

Let's see whether he needed the letter E.

I

From fairest creatures we desire increase,
That thereby beauty's rose might never die,
But as the riper should by time decease,
His tender heir might bear his memory:
But thou, contracted to thine own bright eyes,
Feed'st thy light'st flame with self-substantial fuel,
Making a famine where abundance lies,
Thyself thy foe, to thy sweet self too cruel.
Thou that art now the world's fresh ornament
And only herald to the gaudy spring,
Within thine own bud buriest thy content
And, tender churl, makest waste in niggarding.
  Pity the world, or else this glutton be,
  To eat the world's due, by the grave and thee.

II

When forty winters shall besiege thy brow,
And dig deep trenches in thy beauty's field,
Thy youth's proud livery, so gazed on now,
Will be a tatter'd weed, of small worth held:
Then being ask'd where all thy beauty lies,
Where all the treasure of thy lusty days,
To say, within thine own deep-sunken eyes,
Were an all-eating shame and thriftless praise.
How much more praise deserved thy beauty's use,
If thou couldst answer 'This fair child of mine
Shall sum my count and make my old excuse',
Proving his beauty by succession thine!
  This were to be new made when thou art old,
  And see thy blood warm when thou feel'st it cold.

1 *With Your Good Looks, What About a Child?*

Good-looking folk and animals should pup,
immortalising rosy-blooming glory.
Maturing, I'll pass on, I'll go paunch-up,
and my young sprog will carry on my story.
But you contract your troth with inward look,
nourish your glow with autophagic food,
drying to scarcity your bounty's brook,
your own worst hitman, doing harm, not good.
What! You, this world's outstanding work of art,
you, proclamation of a coming Spring,
bury in your own bud your major part,
wasting good stuff by too tight husbanding!
    For our world's good, nor tomb nor gluttony
    should quaff this birthright of humanity.

Autophagic: consuming his own body.

2 *You Should Pass Your Good Looks On*

With forty annual snows all round your brow
digging war's furrows in your goodly bloom,
your youth's proud swank that folk all look at now
shall shrink, a nugatory wisp of doom.
If anybody asks you: 'Ichabod,
how now, that glory of your lusty past?'
you'll say: 'Look in my hollow orbs.' Good God,
omnivorous dishonour, at what cost!
But look: you, now so fair, might fairly say
This my fair child shall tot up all I do,
and gloss my guilt (if such it is) away,'
proving his looks drawn duly down from you.
    That's how you'd bloom again whilst growing old,
    your blood still warm to sight, though inly cold.

Ichabod (scriptural): 'glory is lost'.

III

Look in thy glass, and tell the face thou viewest
Now is the time that face should form another;
Whose fresh repair if now thou not renewest,
Thou dost beguile the world, unbless some mother.
For where is she so fair whose unear'd womb
Disdains the tillage of thy husbandry?
Or who is he so fond will be the tomb
Of his self-love, to stop posterity?
Thou art thy mother's glass, and she in thee
Calls back the lovely April of her prime:
So thou through windows of thine age shall see
Despite of wrinkles this thy golden time.
    But if thou live, remember'd not to be,
    Die single, and thine image dies with thee.

IV

Unthrifty loveliness, why dost thou spend
Upon thyself thy beauty's legacy?
Nature's bequest gives nothing but doth lend,
And being frank she lends to those are free.
Then, beauteous niggard, why dost thou abuse
The bounteous largess given thee to give?
Profitless usurer, why dost thou use
So great a sum of sums, yet canst not live?
For having traffic with thyself alone,
Thou of thyself thy sweet self dost deceive.
Then how, when nature calls thee to be gone,
What acceptable audit canst thou leave?
    Thy unused beauty must be tomb'd with thee,
    Which, used, lives th' executor to be.

3 You should Start a Family

Look in your glass, inform your physiognomy
that now it ought to plump for duplication:
it's in good nick for doubling its taxonomy.
Don't disappoint us all, don't bilk a matron!
Can any girl with still unfruitful womb
disdain your sowing-drill, your husbandry?
Shall a Narcissus flip from bloom to tomb,
blank his own birthright, foil his family?
You mirror your mama, who looks at you,
calling back youth, and April's days of spring:
so through forthcoming window-glass you too
shall gurn, all wrinkly, at your own off-spring.
    But if you want oblivion, don't marry:
    sign out, 'forgot for good', at mortuary.

*Physiognomy: a human's top front part, with
optical and olfactory organs, mouth, and so on.*

4 You just throw it away

Unthrifty spark, to lavish, on your own
account, that bounty from your mom and poppa!
It's not an outright gift, it's just a loan:
it's rich, and you should pour your cornucopia.
Why, dazzling skinflint, do you misapply
your goods, that bountiful viaticum?
Capitalist without a profit, why
hoard unsustainably so vast a sum?
Your own monopolist, both victim and
originator of improbity,
a natural call for you to go will sound:
what kind of audit will you satisfy?
    Not using it, you doom it to your urn:
    only by using it you'll pass it on.

V

Those hours, that with gentle work did frame
The lovely gaze where every eye doth dwell,
Will play the tyrants to the very same
And that unfair which fairly doth excel:
For never-resting time leads summer on
To hideous winter and confounds him there;
Sap check'd with frost and lusty leaves quite gone,
Beauty o'ersnow'd and bareness every where:
Then, were not summer's distillation left,
A liquid prisoner pent in walls of glass,
Beaut's effect with beauty were bereft,
Nor it nor no remembrance what it was:
  But flowers distill'd though they with winter meet,
  Lease but their show; their substance still lives sweet.

VI

Then let not winter's ragged hand deface
In thee thy summer, ere thou be distill'd:
Make sweet some vial; treasure thou some place
With beauty's treasure, ere it be self-kill'd.
That use is not forbidden usury,
Which happies those that pay the willing loan;
That's for thyself to breed another thee,
Or ten times happier, be it ten for one;
Ten times thyself were happier than thou art,
If ten of thine ten times refigured thee:
Then what could death do, if thou shouldst depart,
Leaving thee living in posterity?
  Be not self-will'd, for thou art much too fair
  To be death's conquest and make worms thine heir.

5 *Warm days turn to cold, you know*

Did passing days with handiwork round out
your glorious gazing orbs, a sight much sought?
Such days will turn tyrannical, no doubt,
and bust that wondrous triumph down to nought.
Chronology ticks on and brings July
to January, strands him in a fix:
sap shrunk by frost, no foliar jollity,
boughs thrawn with snow, stark nudity of sticks.
But distillations of July still stand
as liquid jailbirds caught in walls of glass:
without which, glory couldn't stay at hand,
nor it, nor any sign of what it was.
    Such blooms, dript into jars, in months of cold
    last with looks lost, still fragrantly on hold.

6 *As I said: go to it, lad!*

Don't allow storm and snow with horrid mitt
to smirch your warmth. Bring on your distillation:
fix up a bonny phial, go stashing it
in a good spot. No auto-immolation!
Using it is no sin of usury:
it's joy for all who pay you voluntarily;
and it's for you to spawn and multiply,
in singular or plural, far from sorrily
go triply tripling, tripling too your joy,
triply, your body's cloning copyist:
your burial, though sad, shall not annoy,
by grandsons' warrant, a survivalist.
    So stubborn! Thou art much too fair of form.
    Don't bow to Doom! No bounty for a worm!

VII

Lo! in the orient when the gracious light
Lifts up his burning head, each under eye
Doth homage to his new-appearing sight,
Serving with looks his sacred majesty;
And having climb'd the steep-up heavenly hill,
Resembling strong youth in his middle age,
yet mortal looks adore his beauty still,
Attending on his golden pilgrimage;
But when from highmost pitch, with weary car,
Like feeble age, he reeleth from the day,
The eyes, 'fore duteous, now converted are
From his low tract and look another way:
    So thou, thyself out-going in thy noon,
    Unlook'd on diest, unless thou get a son.

VIII

Music to hear, why hear'st thou music sadly?
Sweets with sweets war not, joy delights in joy.
Why lovest thou that which thou receivest not gladly,
Or else receivest with pleasure thine annoy?
If the true concord of well-tuned sounds,
By unions married, do offend thine ear,
They do but sweetly chide thee, who confounds
In singleness the parts that thou shouldst bear.
Mark how one string, sweet husband to another,
Strikes each in each by mutual ordering,
Resembling sire and child and happy mother
Who all in one, one pleasing note do sing:
    Whose speechless song, being many, seeming one,
    Sings this to thee: 'Thou single wilt prove none.'

7 Suns can fall from glory: so can you

Look towards dawn: you know that gracious light,
day in, day out, lifts up his radiant crown;
all minor orbs do honour to his sight,
submitting to his kingship, bowing down.
And on his climb towards his topmost hill,
outwardly young and strong, though fairly old,
all mortal lights look on, and worship still
as vassals on his pilgrim-path of gold.
Soon from his summit-point with failing car
that poor old man falls fainting from bright day,
and all who dutifully stood turn far
from his low transitus, and look away.
    You too, outgoing proudly in your noon,
    who'll watch you dying? You should spawn a son.

8 Thou art Music! But Sad and Unharmonious

Music, that's you! But you sip music sadly:
sugar is sugar's pal, joy's fond of joy:
you go for it, but don't absorb it gladly,
you absorb joyfully what must annoy.
If a good concord of harmonious sounds,
by unions conjoint, annoys your brain,
your manhood is shown up: it fails, confounds,
singly adrift, that part you should sustain.
Mark how a string plays husband to its ally:
this string plucks that, in mutual harmony,
Just as a mum and dad and child might rally
to sing in unison, a family
    singular-plural, shunning words, this thought:-
    'You on your own will just add up to nought.'

IX

Is it for fear to wet a widow's eye
That thou consumest thyself in single life?
Ah! if thou issueless shalt hap to die.
The world will wail thee, like a makeless wife;
The world will be thy widow and still weep
That thou no form of thee hast left behind,
When every private widow well may keep
By children's eyes her husband's shape in mind.
Look, what an unthrift in the world doth spend
Shifts but his place, for still the world enjoys it;
But beauty's waste hath in the world an end,
And kept unused, the user so destroys it.
    No love toward others in that bosom sits
    That on himself such murderous shame commits.

X

For shame! deny that thou bear'st love to any,
Who for thyself art so unprovident.
Grant, if thou wilt, thou art beloved of many,
But that thou none lovest is most evident;
For thou art so possess'd with murderous hate
That 'gainst thyself thou stick'st not to conspire.
Seeking that beauteous roof to ruinate
Which to repair should be thy chief desire.
O, change thy thought, that I may change my mind!
Shall hate be fairer lodged than gentle love?
Be, as thy presence is, gracious and kind,
Or to thyself at least kind-hearted prove:
    Make thee another self, for love of me,
    That beauty still may live in thine or thee.

9 *Worrying about a widow crying for you?*

Is this your worry - might your widow cry?
O solitary soul, autophagous!
What if you pass away without small fry?
This world will mourn, your consort azygous,
this world, your widow, constantly shall sorrow
that you laid down no copy, as you should,
whilst any two-bit widow's apt to borrow
husband's old form from orbs of growing brood.
All that an unthrift in this world lays out
stays on in circulation, to our profit;
but good looks, thrown away, won't hang about:
not using's losing; lord it, don't lay off it!
    No kind compassion in that bosom sits
    that such a suicidal wrong commits.

Azygous: having no yoking, no consort.

10 *So you don't want anybody? Think again!*

Shocking! You say you do not go for any
of us; you don't look out (you mug) for you;
grant, if you will, you light a lamp for many:
you fancy nobody, that's what you do.
Your animus is full of odium,
it's mortal: what an arrant autoblapt!
You aim to smash that glorious atrium:
you should maintain it: that ambition's apt.
Adjust your thought, and I'll adjust my mind:
should loathing's domus vanquish that of loving?
Match your good looks: act gracious, turn out kind,
philanthropist or autophiliac proving.
    Run off a copy of your glory, do,
    just for Will, saving it in yours or you.

Blapto, I harm; philia, loving: words known to Plato.
Latin words: animus, spirit; odium, loathing;
atrium, high hall; domus, a building for living in.

XI

As fast as thou shalt wane, so fast thou growest
In one of thine, from that which thou departest;
And that fresh blood which youngly thou bestowest
Thou mayst call thine when thou from youth convertest.
Herein lives wisdom, beauty and increase:
Without this, folly, age and cold decay:
If all were minded so, the times should cease
And threescore year would make the world away.
Let those whom Nature hath not made for store,
Harsh, featureless and rude, barrenly perish:
Look, whom she best endow'd she gave the more;
Which bounteous gift thou shouldst in bounty cherish:
    She carved thee for her seal, and meant thereby
    Thou shouldst print more, not let that copy die.

XII

When I do count the clock that tells the time,
And see the brave day sunk in hideous night;
When I behold the violet past prime,
And sable curls all silver'd o'er with white;
When lofty trees I see barren of leaves
Which erst from heat did canopy the herd,
And summer's green all girded up in sheaves
Borne on the bier with white and bristly beard,
Then of thy beauty do I question make,
That thou among the wastes of time must go,
Since sweets and beauties do themselves forsake
And die as fast as they see others grow;
    And nothing 'gainst Time's scythe can make defence
    Save breed, to brave him when he takes thee hence.

11 So good-looking, you should print a Copy

As fast as you shall wilt, you'll also grow
in your own brood, to whom you'll bid goodby,
and that blood, issuing from your youthful glow,
you can call yours, in your maturity.
It's wisdom, cash at bank, and joy on top:
without it, foolish ruin, cold and chill:
if all mankind thought your way, clocks would stop,
in half a gross of Aprils, worlds fall still.
Folk not worth saving, misprints roughly wrought,
can fill a lowly and unfruitful shroud;
look at your wondrous gifts! Do what you ought,
pass your gift on, solicitously proud.
 Such art, such bounty's not for you to banish:
 so, print again! That copy must not vanish.

12 All Things Must Pass: so what about it?

I look at clocks and count up hour on hour
and watch proud day sink down in ugly night,
I look at many a worn-out gillyflow'r
and at black curls awash with hoary blight;
I look at lofty larch that lost its crown,
which from hot sun did canopy our flocks,
and August's virid bounty all knit down,
sad cartload sprouting pallid bristly locks:
and I think hard about your famous form,
that you at last in lapsing voids must go:
what's glorious and joyful must disarm
and finish, fast as young arrivals grow;
 and nothing can ward off that scything swing
 but sprogs, to vaunt against its harrowing.

XIII

O, that you were yourself! but, love, you are
No longer yours than you yourself here live:
Against this coming end you should prepare,
And your sweet semblance to some other give.
So should that beauty which you hold in lease
Find no determination: then you were
Yourself again after yourself's decease,
When your sweet issue your sweet form should bear.
Who lets so fair a house fall to decay,
Which husbandry in honour might uphold
Against the stormy gusts of winter's day
And barren rage of death's eternal cold?
   O, none but unthrifts! Dear my love, you know
   You had a father: let your son say so.

XIV

Not from the stars do I my judgment pluck;
And yet methinks I have astronomy,
But not to tell of good or evil luck,
Of plagues, of dearths, or seasons' quality;
Nor can I fortune to brief minutes tell
Pointing to each his thunder, rain and wind,
Or say with princes if it shall go well,
By oft predict that I in heaven find:
But from thine eyes my knowledge I derive,
And, constant stars, in them I read such art
As truth and beauty shall together thrive,
If from thyself to store thou wouldst convert;
   Or else of thee this I prognosticate:
   Thy end is truth's and beauty's doom and date.

13 *How to last: pass good looks on to a son*

If only you could last! But, chuck, you'll vanish,
last only just as long as you stay living.
You ought to guard against that coming finish,
pass on your good looks, bountifully giving!
So shall that fair form which you hold on loan
avoid withdrawal, though you pass away:
you can outlast your quiddity, stay on:
your palmy child prolongs your palmy day.
Who would allow high-standard build to fall,
which husbandry in honour might uphold
against unstinting storm, and frost, and all
unfruitful fury of long mortal cold?
    Only an unthrift! Darling, as you know,
    you had a dad: why can't your son say so?

14 *Your Two Bright Optic Orbs*

Not out of stars do I opinions pluck;
still, I can claim to know astrology,
though not to fathom good or awful luck,
nor blight, starvation, climatology;
nor can I pinpoint hourly on my clock
an individual's rain or wind or storm;
for politicians, too, I can't unlock
good karma, for sky-writing won't inform.
No, but your two bright optics! – my two books,
two constant stars, in which I scan such art:
triumph of truth and magical good looks,
if you go out to stud, and play your part;
    if not, I say all truth attains its doom,
    all good looks fail, that hour you fill your tomb.

XV

When I consider every thing that grows
Holds in perfection but a little moment,
That this huge stage presenteth nought but shows
Whereon the stars in secret influence comment;
When I perceive that men as plants increase,
Cheered and check'd even by the self-same sky,
Vaunt in their youthful sap, at height decrease,
And wear their brave state out of memory;
Then the conceit of this inconstant stay
Sets you most rich in youth before my sight,
Where wasteful Time debateth with Decay,
To change your day of youth to sullied night;
  And all in war with Time for love of you,
  As he takes from you, I engraft you new.

XVI

But wherefore do not you a mightier way
Make war upon this bloody tyrant, Time?
And fortify yourself in your decay
With means more blessed than my barren rhyme?
Now stand you on the top of happy hours,
And many maiden gardens yet unset
With virtuous wish would bear your living flowers,
Much liker than your painted counterfeit:
So should the lines of life that life repair,
Which this, Time's pencil, or my pupil pen,
Neither in inward worth nor outward fair,
Can make you live yourself in eyes of men.
  To give away yourself keeps yourself still,
  And you must live, drawn by your own sweet skill.

15 Nothing lasts long: for you, I'm fighting Anno Domini.

I think about it: anything that grows
holds its top notch for just a short half-day,
and this Big Top can only put on shows:
stars, by astrology, know what to say.
Mankind grows as do plants, which sun and rain
bring on - or not - with stars and clouds and wind:
vaunts youthful sap, but must at last sink down,
till all that pomp's worn out, and out of mind.
I think about this most inconstant stay:
you swim, most rich in youth, into my sight,
and rot and Anno Domini parlay
to switch your day of youth to filthy night,
    and I'm at war with him for loving you.
    That ruffian strims you - but I'm grafting too.

16 Having a child: that's your survival. Not my words!

Why don't you just go up a notch or two
fighting this tyrant, Anno Domini!
Stand firm and strong against what ruins you:
your skills trump my unfruitful artistry.
Such happy hours, of which you stand on top!
how many virgin orchards, still unlaid,
with virtuous wish would sprout your living crop,
an avatar not wrought by paint's poor aid.
Combat your living loss with living growth!
Not Anno's stylus, nor my own poor scratch,
can draw your outward looks nor inward worth,
your living portrait, right for all who watch.
    Auto-donation shall support you still:
    survival's yours, drawn by your own straight skill.

XVII

Who will believe my verse in time to come,
If it were fill'd with your most high deserts?
Though yet, heaven knows, it is but as a tomb
Which hides your life and shows not half your parts.
 If I could write the beauty of your eyes
And in fresh numbers number all your graces,
The age to come would say 'This poet lies:
Such heavenly touches ne'er touch'd earthly faces.'
So should my papers yellow'd with their age
Be scorn'd like old men of less truth than tongue,
And your true rights be term'd a poet's rage
And stretched metre of an antique song:
   But were some child of yours alive that time,
   You should live twice; in it and in my rhyme.

XVIII

Shall I compare thee to a summer's day?
Thou art more lovely and more temperate:
Rough winds do shake the darling buds of May,
And summer's lease hath all too short a date:
Sometime too hot the eye of heaven shines,
And often is his gold complexion dimm'd;
And every fair from fair sometime declines,
By chance or nature's changing course untrimm'd;
But thy eternal summer shall not fade
Nor lose possession of that fair thou owest;
Nor shall Death brag thou wander'st in his shade,
When in eternal lines to time thou growest:
   So long as men can breathe or eyes can see,
   So long lives this and this gives life to thee.

17 Do it, as a corroboration of my account!

Who will lap up my script in far-off days,
if I proclaim your worth in its totality?
- a script that's nothing but a tomb, God knows,
shrouding your vigour, hiding half your quality.
Could I in cool account count all, and could
I just jot down how bright your iris is,
oh, far-off days would say 'This bard's no good:
such glorious tints can touch no mortal phiz.'
So my hard copy, wilting, wan, would fall
flat as a dotard, gabbling randomly:
'an old bard's lunacy': so folk would call
your rightful worth: a rambling rhapsody.
　　But if your child is living at that timing,
　　you'll blossom, by your child and by my rhyming.

Phiz: short for physiognomy.

18 Comparing you with a day
　　　probably in July or August

I'll put you up against a balmy day...
You win on looks. Not cold, and not too warm.
Winds cut up rough with darling buds of May;
a two-month contract can't supply much balm.
Dog-days in August turn to burning hot,
or may contrarily grow all too dim;
and all fair fowls fall foul of you-know-what,
thrown by bad luck, or sunspots, out of trim.
But your hot days will last and last and last,
maintaining tiptop form with full control;
nor shall morticians brag of shadows cast
across your path. My words shall grow your soul.
　　Mankind may gasp and gawp, unstoppably:
　　I sign this gift, your immortality.

XIX

Devouring Time, blunt thou the lion's paws,
And make the earth devour her own sweet brood;
Pluck the keen teeth from the fierce tiger's jaws,
And burn the long-lived phoenix in her blood;
Make glad and sorry seasons as thou fleets,
And do whate'er thou wilt, swift-footed Time,
To the wide world and all her fading sweets;
But I forbid thee one most heinous crime:
O, carve not with thy hours my love's fair brow,
Nor draw no lines there with thine antique pen;
Him in thy course untainted do allow
For beauty's pattern to succeeding men.
    Yet, do thy worst, old Time: despite thy wrong,
    My love shall in my verse ever live young.

XX

A woman's face with Nature's own hand painted
Hast thou, the master-mistress of my passion;
A woman's gentle heart, but not acquainted
With shifting change, as is false women's fashion;
An eye more bright than theirs, less false in rolling,
Gilding the object whereupon it gazeth;
A man in hue, all 'hues' in his controlling,
Much steals men's eyes and women's souls amazeth.
And for a woman wert thou first created;
Till Nature, as she wrought thee, fell a-doting,
And by addition me of thee defeated,
By adding one thing to my purpose nothing.
    But since she prick'd thee out for women's pleasure,
    Mine be thy love and thy love's use their treasure.

19 Don't Touch My Darling

You glutton, Anno Domini! Go blunt
a lion's paws; bid Cronos gulp his brood;
pull molars out of big cats' mouths, and hunt
a mythic bird you'll roast in its own blood;
whiz past, inflicting pains or sowing joys:
all that you wish, 'Fast Forward', you may do
to all our world and all its fading toys.
But know that this misconduct is taboo:
don't scratch my darling's brow with roughshod hours;
no scribbling on it with your worn-out nibs.
Don't stain or mark this morning star of ours,
a mark to mark, not just for Adam's ribs...
    Oh, do your worst, old fool! For all your wrong,
    my darling's bloom shall flourish in my song.

20 A Woman's Good Looks on a Man!

A woman's phiz – it's natural, no paint –
is yours, my king, first lady of my passion;
a woman's soft midpoint, that don't acquaint
shifting mutation, dubious woman's fashion;
orbs bright as woman's, not absurdly rolling,
but gilding anything you Wi-Sh (!) to zoom on;
a man in tints all H(!)ints in his controlling,
purloining man-orbs, spooking souls of woman:
a form that as a woman first was cast,
until Natura, forming you but doting,
by an addition of a phalloplast
saw off my vivid wish, and I got nothing.
    You by such pricking-out grant all girls joy,
    loving Yours Truly, all girls' darling boy.

XXI

So is it not with me as with that Muse
Stirr'd by a painted beauty to his verse,
Who heaven itself for ornament doth use
And every fair with his fair doth rehearse
Making a couplement of proud compare,
With sun and moon, with earth and sea's rich gems,
With April's first-born flowers, and all things rare
That heaven's air in this huge rondure hems.
O let me, true in love, but truly write,
And then believe me, my love is as fair
As any mother's child, though not so bright
As those gold candles fix'd in heaven's air:
   Let them say more that like of hearsay well;
   I will not praise that purpose not to sell.

XXII

My glass shall not persuade me I am old,
So long as youth and thou are of one date;
But when in thee time's furrows I behold,
Then look I death my days should expiate.
For all that beauty that doth cover thee
Is but the seemly raiment of my heart,
Which in thy breast doth live, as thine in me:
How can I then be elder than thou art?
O, therefore, love, be of thyself so wary
As I, not for myself, but for thee will;
Bearing thy heart, which I will keep so chary
As tender nurse her babe from faring ill.
   Presume not on thy heart when mine is slain;
   Thou gavest me thine, not to give back again.

21 I Say it Straight, I don't Gild your Lily.

I am not such as any rhyming fool
caught up in fancy paintwork of his writing,
who finds in utmost sky what's worshipful,
and pits his fair against all fairs by flyting,
comparing two by two with moon and sun,
rich joys of land and flood, a first-born bloom
of April, anything in fact that's unusual, within our skyball's mighty room.
Truth! For I'm truly loving. Truth and light!
Trust anything I say! My chuck is fair
as any momma's child, though not so bright
as lamps of gold that hang aloft i' th' air.
    Folk may add much, if folk go in for talking:
    I will not lay it on: I am not hawking.

Flyting: bards in antagonistic combat: a Slam.

22 I'm as Young as You; Our Mutual Cordiality

Proving I'm old? That's what my glass can't do,
so long as you and youth show synchrony:
but if I spot a furrow-mark on you,
I brood on shriving and mortality.
Your good looks wrap around you, form a gown,
draping my cardiac part, that lurks within,
inhabiting your bosom, as your own
inhabits my own bosom: I'm your twin,
as young as you. So, sonny boy, stay canny,
just as I altruistically will,
cradling your *carum cor*, a wary nanny
that stops a darling baby falling ill.
    Don't count on yours, though, if my own is slain:
    it was your gift: it can't go back again.

*Latin: darling midpoint, our vital bodily organ.

XXIII

As an unperfect actor on the stage
Who with his fear is put besides his part,
Or some fierce thing replete with too much rage,
Whose strength's abundance weakens his own heart.
So I, for fear of trust, forget to say
The perfect ceremony of love's rite,
And in mine own love's strength seem to decay,
O'ercharged with burden of mine own love's might.
O, let my books be then the eloquence
And dumb presagers of my speaking breast,
Who plead for love and look for recompense
More than that tongue that more hath more express'd.
   O, learn to read what silent love hath writ:
   To hear with eyes belongs to love's fine wit.

XXIV

Mine eye hath play'd the painter and hath stell'd
Thy beauty's form in table of my heart;
My body is the frame wherein 'tis held,
And perspective it is the painter's art.
For through the painter must you see his skill,
To find where your true image pictured lies;
Which in my bosom's shop is hanging still,
That hath his windows glazed with thine eyes.
Now see what good turns eyes for eyes have done:
Mine eyes have drawn thy shape, and thine for me
Are windows to my breast, where-through the sun
Delights to peep, to gaze therein on thee;
   Yet eyes this cunning want to grace their art;
   They draw but what they see, know not the heart.

23 I can't say it! It's up to my Books to say it.

An actor in a play who's lost his words
is shock-struck, not inhabiting his part;
an animal or man too furious hoards
too much strong blood, his cardiac pump won't start.
So I, afraid to trust, must fail to say
full liturgy of loving's ritual,
loving so strongly that I faint away,
can't lift my monstrous loving load at all.
So it's my books must hook my thoughts on his,
portraying dumbly what my soul would cry:
orator-books call in my loan of bliss,
out-talking all my throat's capacity.
    So, study adoration's tacit writ:
    visual's as good as audiovisual wit.

24 My Visual Portrayal of You

My gazing orb with paintbrush and with art
has caught your pomp and glory, *io lo giuro*;
my body is your mount, my inmost part
your canvas. What a riot of †*chiaroscuro*!
Light up this artist, fossick through his skill,
to find your portrait, your illuminating,
which in my bosom's shop is hanging still,
your gazing orbs its glassy window-glazing.
Now look what good turns orbs for orbs can do:
my orbs did draw your contours: yours in turn
form windows for my bosom, all shot through
with shafts of sun, that pry, and softly burn!
    But orbs of sight lack insight, which with art
    draw outward things, but miss our inward part.

* Italian for 'by my oath'. † Ditto for 'light-and-dark'.

XXV

Let those who are in favour with their stars
Of public honour and proud titles boast,
Whilst I, whom fortune of such triumph bars,
Unlook'd for joy in that I honour most.
Great princes' favourites their fair leaves spread
But as the marigold at the sun's eye,
And in themselves their pride lies buried,
For at a frown they in their glory die.
The painful warrior famoused for fight,
After a thousand victories once foil'd,
Is from the book of honour razed quite,
And all the rest forgot for which he toil'd:
    Then happy I, that love and am beloved
    Where I may not remove nor be removed.

XXVI

Lord of my love, to whom in vassalage
Thy merit hath my duty strongly knit,
To thee I send this written embassage,
To witness duty, not to show my wit:
Duty so great, which wit so poor as mine
May make seem bare, in wanting words to show it,
But that I hope some good conceit of thine
In thy soul's thought, all naked, will bestow it;
Till whatsoever star that guides my moving
Points on me graciously with fair aspect
And puts apparel on my tatter'd loving,
To show me worthy of thy sweet respect:
    Then may I dare to boast how I do love thee;
    Till then not show my head where thou mayst prove me.

25 Honours may not Last – I'm Happy with You

All you who stand in favour with your stars,
of gongs and public honours you may boast,
whilst I, whom ill-luck from such triumph bars,
by jingo! joy in what I honour most.
In a king's favour many a man may bloom
as much as might a sunlit marigold:
but inwardly his pomp is in its tomb,
and at a frown, that's it! his glory's cold.
A warrior, glorious in bout and rout,
adds to his thousandth victory a loss:
from honour's book harsh hands will scratch him out,
his toil's forgot, and all his work is dross.
   I'm happy with our mutual gifts of loving,
   and happy, that my loving knows no moving.

26 O My Lord, Sir, I'm Simply Not Up To It!

Lord of my loving, I'm your vassal who
is bound by loyalty most strongly knit;
I post this intimation off to you
by way of duty, not to show my wit:
duty so vast, which wit so poor as ours
may strip right down, in wanting words to show it,
but with good luck, a fitting thought of yours
into your soul's mind, all unclad, will stow it.
Until that high star which controls my moving
points to my brow with gracious favour fair,
and smartly garbs my ragamuffin loving,
showing I'm worth a point in your good quair:
   that day, I'll boast of you and of my loving;
   but won't pop up, just now, to risk your proving.

Quair (Scottish): book.

XXVII

Weary with toil, I haste me to my bed,
The dear repose for limbs with travel tired;
But then begins a journey in my head,
To work my mind, when body's work's expired:
For then my thoughts, from far where I abide,
Intend a zealous pilgrimage to thee,
And keep my drooping eyelids open wide,
Looking on darkness which the blind do see:
Save that my soul's imaginary sight
Presents thy shadow to my sightless view,
Which, like a jewel hung in ghastly night,
Makes black night beauteous and her old face new.
   Lo! thus, by day my limbs, by night my mind,
    For thee and for myself no quiet find.

XXVIII

How can I then return in happy plight,
That am debarr'd the benefit of rest?
When day's oppression is not eased by night,
But day by night, and night by day, oppress'd?
And each, though enemies to either's reign,
Do in consent shake hands to torture me;
The one by toil, the other to complain
How far I toil, still farther off from thee.
I tell the day, to please them thou art bright
And dost him grace when clouds do blot the heaven:
So flatter I the swart-complexion'd night,
When sparkling stars twire not thou gild'st the even.
   But day doth daily draw my sorrows longer
    And night doth nightly make grief's strength seem stronger.

27 Can't Stop Thinking of You

Worn out with toil I hurry to my cot,
soothing my limbs, from travail's cart stood down;
but in my skull it's go go go, *God wot! -
I work my mind, now body-work is flown.
For it's my thoughts, from this far distant land,
that long to tramp on pilgrims' way to you,
propping my drooping lids still vigilant,
that look at pitch-black night, as blind folks do.
Only my soul's imaginary sight
submits your shadow to my purblind vision:
and that's a diamond hung in ghastly night,
adorning night, upgrading its condition.
    My limbs may try by day, by night my mind:
    tranquillity for two, I cannot find.

*This pair of words is indisputably by Sir Francis Bacon,
and not by Lord Oxford. (Bacon, or Oxford, is thought of
by a minority as shadowy author of all this coruscation.)

28 Night and Day, still Sorrowing.

How can I turn again in happy plight,
that am shut out from all tranquillity?
Day's tyranny is not brought down by night:
day groans in night's, night in day's tyranny:
this pair, though mutual in hostility,
shook hands to put yours truly on a rack,
day by hard toil, night by this litany:
I'm far from you, I'm toiling, falling back!
I talk with day, I say you'll bring him light,
gracing him, if clouds blot absconding sky;
I lay it on as much for swarthy night:
if sparkling stars don't gild, you shall supply.
    But daily day draws out my sorrows long,
    which nightly night protracts, both long and strong.

XXIX

When, in disgrace with fortune and men's eyes,
I all alone beweep my outcast state
And trouble deaf heaven with my bootless cries
And look upon myself and curse my fate,
Wishing me like to one more rich in hope,
Featured like him, like him with friends possess'd,
Desiring this man's art and that man's scope,
With what I most enjoy contented least;
Yet in these thoughts myself almost despising,
Haply I think on thee, and then my state,
Like to the lark at break of day arising
From sullen earth, sings hymns at heaven's gate;
    For thy sweet love remember'd such wealth brings
    That then I scorn to change my state with kings.

XXX

When to the sessions of sweet silent thought
I summon up remembrance of things past,
I sigh the lack of many a thing I sought,
And with old woes new wail my dear time's waste:
Then can I drown an eye, unused to flow,
For precious friends hid in death's dateless night,
And weep afresh love's long since cancell'd woe,
And moan the expense of many a vanish'd sight:
Then can I grieve at grievances foregone,
And heavily from woe to woe tell o'er
The sad account of fore-bemoaned moan,
Which I new pay as if not paid before.
    But if the while I think on thee, dear friend,
    All losses are restored and sorrows end.

29 I'm out of luck...until I think of you

I'm out of luck and out of favour too.
I mourn my solitary, sad condition,
annoying God with vapid boo hoo hoo,
angry about my pitiful position.
If only I could match a lucky man,
a man who has good looks and lots of pals,
a man of parts and skills, a man who can!
I spurn my normal joys and rituals.
I know it's all disgusting; but what's this?
I think of you, and my condition soars,
day dawns, I quit dull ground, and fly to bliss,
a skylark, trilling hymns at bliss's doors.
 Thoughts of your warmth! I'm rich, I'm flourishing,
 I wouldn't swap my station with a king.

30 Writing Off Past Pains

Now and again I sit in soundproof thought
and summon up (Proust's parrot-cry) things past:
I sigh for lack of many things I sought:
updating pains, I mourn for hours I lost.
I flood my thirsty ducts, that drown forlorn,
for staunch amigos hid in mortal night,
and cry for sorrows long ago outworn,
and moan my loss of many a long-lost sight.
I'm sad at what was sad, though now it's not,
start listing pains untold and pains unsaid,
accounting still for moans of which I'm shot,
and pay again, as if I hadn't paid.
 But oh, *mio caro, if I think of you,
 all loss is null and void, all sorrow too.

*Italian. I won't insult you with a translation.

XXXI

Thy bosom is endeared with all hearts,
Which I by lacking have supposed dead,
And there reigns love and all love's loving parts,
And all those friends which I thought buried.
How many a holy and obsequious tear
Hath dear religious love stol'n from mine eye
As interest of the dead, which now appear
But things removed that hidden in thee lie!
Thou art the grave where buried love doth live,
Hung with the trophies of my lovers gone,
Who all their parts of me to thee did give;
That due of many now is thine alone:
    Their images I loved I view in thee,
    And thou, all they, hast all the all of me.

XXXII

If thou survive my well-contented day,
When that churl Death my bones with dust shall cover,
And shalt by fortune once more re-survey
These poor rude lines of thy deceased lover,
Compare them with the bettering of the time,
And though they be outstripp'd by every pen,
Reserve them for my love, not for their rhyme,
Exceeded by the height of happier men.
O, then vouchsafe me but this loving thought:
'Had my friend's Muse grown with this growing age,
A dearer birth than this his love had brought,
To march in ranks of better equipage:
    But since he died and poets better prove,
    Theirs for their style I'll read, his for his love.'

31 *All my old darlings got caught up in you.*

Your bosom's lovably conjoint with all
bosoms which, lacking, I'd put down as bust;
Cupid's its lord; and Cupid's loving ball
of parts; and many a jo I thought was dust.
How many a worshipful and holy drop
ran down by pious loving to my chin:
drops drawn by mortals past, which now pop up
as part of you, a part that lurks within!
Laid out in you, all my long-lost amours,
you burial-vault, hung round with trophy-swags!
So many parts of Will now count as yours,
brought in from many to fill out your bags.
    Portrayals of my darlings now in you
    I savour; yours is all my total, too.

Jo (Scottish): darling, bosom pal, amigo, chum.

32 *Bards may outbard my Writing,*
but not my Loving.

If you outlast my fully paid-up days,
on which churl Charon loads my shanks with dust,
and luckily shall study, as always,
this poor rough scribbling of your swain long-lost,
match it against improving innovation:
bank it, though it falls short of coming bards,
just for my loving, not for composition,
lacking sublimity of rivals' words.
On that day grant your Will this loving thought:
'Had my pal's art grown in this brilliant way,
what wondrous offspring had his passion brought,
to march in ranks of glorious display:
    but, mortal coil! and bards now skilful proving,
    I'll study such for art, and him for loving.'

Charon: grim boatman who, for two obols (small coins),
would row you across Styx's cold flood, but not back again.

XXXIII

Full many a glorious morning have I seen
Flatter the mountain-tops with sovereign eye,
Kissing with golden face the meadows green,
Gilding pale streams with heavenly alchemy;
Anon permit the basest clouds to ride
With ugly rack on his celestial face,
And from the forlorn world his visage hide,
Stealing unseen to west with this disgrace:
Even so my sun one early morn did shine
With all-triumphant splendor on my brow
But out, alack! he was but one hour mine;
The region cloud hath mask'd him from me now.
   Yet him for this my love no whit disdaineth;
   Suns of the world may stain when heaven's sun staineth.

XXXIV

Why didst thou promise such a beauteous day,
And make me travel forth without my cloak,
To let base clouds o'ertake me in my way,
Hiding thy bravery in their rotten smoke?
'Tis not enough that through the cloud thou break
To dry the rain on my storm-beaten face,
For no man well of such a salve can speak
That heals the wound and cures not the disgrace:
Nor can thy shame give physic to my grief;
Though thou repent, yet I have still the loss:
The offender's sorrow lends but weak relief
To him that bears the strong offence's cross.
   Ah! but those tears are pearl which thy love sheds,
   And they are rich and ransom all ill deeds.

33 Clouds can block sunlight, including my own..., But, OK !

Full many a glorious morning did I spot,
touching up mountain-tops with kingly smirk,
kissing with lips of gold an upland plot,
gilding wan brooks with sky-high wizard-work,
allow too soon disgusting clouds to mount
with ugly trail on his Olympian phiz,
withdrawing from our mournful world his front,
slinking to couch, such gross dishonour his:
just so, I saw my own sun shining bright
with all-triumphant glory on my brow;
but out, alas, alack! hid from my sight
in just an hour, by cloud's occlusion now.
    Too bad! To worship him I don't disdain:
     sun stains on high, our own suns too may stain.

34 Thanks to You, I got Caught in a Rainstorm

Why did you talk about a sunny day?
Just look! I got caught out without my hat!
Whom nasty clouds waylaid along my way,
hiding your glory in a putrid splat.
It isn't up to scratch, you, bright and calm,
drying rain off my storm-struck ocular:
nobody has good words for any balm
that calms a wound but cannot fix a scar.
Nor is your blush a physick for my pain,
and your apology won't halt my loss:
your guilty sorrow is my puny gain,
I carry such a strong misdoing's cross.
    Most lustrous opals, though, your loving spills,
     and all so rich, to ransom all my ills.

XXXV

No more be grieved at that which thou hast done:
Roses have thorns, and silver fountains mud;
Clouds and eclipses stain both moon and sun,
And loathsome canker lives in sweetest bud.
All men make faults, and even I in this,
Authorizing thy trespass with compare,
Myself corrupting, salving thy amiss,
Excusing thy sins more than thy sins are;
For to thy sensual fault I bring in sense--
Thy adverse party is thy advocate--
And 'gainst myself a lawful plea commence:
Such civil war is in my love and hate
    That I an accessary needs must be
    To that sweet thief which sourly robs from me.

XXXVI

Let me confess that we two must be twain,
Although our undivided loves are one:
So shall those blots that do with me remain
Without thy help by me be borne alone.
In our two loves there is but one respect,
Though in our lives a separable spite,
Which though it alter not love's sole effect,
Yet doth it steal sweet hours from love's delight.
I may not evermore acknowledge thee,
Lest my bewailed guilt should do thee shame,
Nor thou with public kindness honour me,
Unless thou take that honour from thy name:
    But do not so; I love thee in such sort
    As, thou being mine, mine is thy good report.

35 *You did wrong: and I do wrong,*
   in justifying you.

Don't worry now about your sin, my son:
on rosy shrubs lurk thorns, in fountains mud:
clouds and occlusions stain both moon and sun,
and grisly blight is found in goodly bud.
All guys do wrong, and I do wrong in this,
condoning your bad action by comparing:
spoil my own book, your downfall to dismiss,
forgiving you too much, too lightly sparing.
Your fault was bodily: I bring in brain.
Opposing you, it's you I'm vouching for:
your plaintiff's word in court compounds your gain!
Loving and hating, I'm in civil war;
    and so I aid and comfort, as I must,
     that darling horrid burglar of my trust.

36 *Two of us, living apart, but sharing...*

I know that you and I add up to two,
for all our loving's unsplit unity:
and so my blots, which cannot sully you,
stay as my load, my liability.
Your and my loving own a common goal,
our living is, alas, fissiparous:
this may not impact on our troth at all,
but think what hours of joy it nicks from us!
I cannot constantly lay claim to you:
my guilt (I'm sorry now!) would smirch your glory;
nor can you publicly pay honour to
your Will, without dishonouring your story.
    Don't do it, though: you know my caring humour:
    I hold you tight, and hold off ugly rumour.

XXXVII

As a decrepit father takes delight
To see his active child do deeds of youth,
So I, made lame by fortune's dearest spite,
Take all my comfort of thy worth and truth.
For whether beauty, birth, or wealth, or wit,
Or any of these all, or all, or more,
Entitled in thy parts do crowned sit,
I make my love engrafted to this store:
So then I am not lame, poor, nor despised,
Whilst that this shadow doth such substance give
That I in thy abundance am sufficed
And by a part of all thy glory live.
    Look, what is best, that best I wish in thee:
    This wish I have; then ten times happy me!

XXXVIII

How can my Muse want subject to invent,
While thou dost breathe, that pour'st into my verse
Thine own sweet argument, too excellent
For every vulgar paper to rehearse?
O, give thyself the thanks, if aught in me
Worthy perusal stand against thy sight;
For who's so dumb that cannot write to thee,
When thou thyself dost give invention light?
Be thou the tenth Muse, ten times more in worth
Than those old nine which rhymers invocate;
And he that calls on thee, let him bring forth
Eternal numbers to outlive long date.
    If my slight Muse do please these curious days,
    The pain be mine, but thine shall be the praise.

37 *Vicarious Joy, that's what it is*

Just as a poor old dad looks on with joy
watching his child do stirring acts of youth,
so I, whilst hobbling with bad luck's annoy,
obtain my comfort from your worth and truth.
No odds if looks or birth or gold or wit,
or any of this list, or all, or what,
squat in your parts as rightful kings may sit;
I graft my admiration to your glut.
So I'm no limping butt of sad disdain,
but in your shadow find substantial thriving,
which your abounding vigour can sustain:
on part of all your glory I'm surviving.
    For you, I only wish top quality.
    To my joy's logarithm, add unity!

*Adding unity to a logarithm of any amount is tantamount to
multiplying that amount by a third of thirty, a fifth of fifty...*

38 *With You as Inspiration, I Can't Miss*

How can my inspiration fail, if thou art living
and pour'st into my compositions thy
own darling script, too good for any striving
vulgarian to match in rivalry?
O! thank your own fair form, if I at all
stand worthy of assay against your sight;
for who's so dumb that cannot work a small
word about you, a makar's shining light?
You, last Parnassian, *dix fois plus* in worth
than songbirds' tripling trios of old days:
I call on you to grant that I bring forth
 surviving compositions, lasting lays.
    If my slight skills win through in probing hours,
    I must work hard; all kudos, though, is yours.

Makar: Scots bard.
Parnasssian: lady inspiring artists from on high.

XXXIX

O, how thy worth with manners may I sing,
When thou art all the better part of me?
What can mine own praise to mine own self bring?
And what is 't but mine own when I praise thee?
Even for this let us divided live,
And our dear love lose name of single one,
That by this separation I may give
That due to thee which thou deservest alone.
O absence, what a torment wouldst thou prove,
Were it not thy sour leisure gave sweet leave
To entertain the time with thoughts of love,
Which time and thoughts so sweetly doth deceive,
   And that thou teachest how to make one twain,
   By praising him here who doth hence remain!

XL

Take all my loves, my love, yea, take them all;
What hast thou then more than thou hadst before?
No love, my love, that thou mayst true love call;
All mine was thine before thou hadst this more.
Then if for my love thou my love receivest
I cannot blame thee for my love thou usest;
But yet be blamed, if thou thyself deceivest
By wilful taste of what thyself refusest.
I do forgive thy robbery, gentle thief,
Although thou steal thee all my poverty;
And yet, love knows, it is a greater grief
To bear love's wrong than hate's known injury.
   Lascivious grace, in whom all ill well shows,
   Kill me with spites; yet we must not be foes.

39 Splitting and Still Singing About You

About thy worth, how can I aptly sing,
knowing that thou art all my major part?
What can my praising to my profit bring?
It's all my own, if you attract my art.
So you and I should go our ways and split,
and drop our loving's famous unity,
so I can honour you with all that's fit,
owing, if not to you, to nobody.
Apart! How agonising that could work
out! But sour solitary hours allow
to think amusing loving thoughts, that lurk,
 thoughts and hours too, in ambush soft; and thou
    show'st forth instruction, how I'd split in two,
    praising, *in situ*, my far distant you.

40 Go on! Rob Your Poor Will Blind!

Filch all my darlings, darling! Filch away!
So what's now yours, that up to now was not,
darling? No loving, you can truly say:
my loving was all yours, without this lot.
You took my darling, swapping for my loving,
shafting my loving and my darling too:
OK, but, wilful fool! I'm disapproving,
if you grab what you know's not right for you.
I pardon you this burglary, Sir Crook,
although you filch my total bankruptcy.
Darling! A darling's wrong I cannot brook:
I'd opt for odium's known injury.
    Lascivious glory! Shining fount of ill!
    Kill Will, most vicious, but my darling still.

XLI

Those petty wrongs that liberty commits,
When I am sometime absent from thy heart,
Thy beauty and thy years full well befits,
For still temptation follows where thou art.
Gentle thou art and therefore to be won,
Beauteous thou art, therefore to be assailed;
And when a woman woos, what woman's son
Will sourly leave her till she have prevailed?
Ay me! but yet thou mightest my seat forbear,
And chide thy beauty and thy straying youth,
Who lead thee in their riot even there
Where thou art forced to break a twofold truth,
*   Hers by thy beauty tempting her to thee,*
*   Thine, by thy beauty being false to me.*

XLII

That thou hast her, it is not all my grief,
And yet it may be said I loved her dearly;
That she hath thee, is of my wailing chief,
A loss in love that touches me more nearly.
Loving offenders, thus I will excuse ye:
Thou dost love her, because thou knowst I love her;
And for my sake even so doth she abuse me,
Suffering my friend for my sake to approve her.
If I lose thee, my loss is my love's gain,
And losing her, my friend hath found that loss;
Both find each other, and I lose both twain,
And both for my sake lay on me this cross:
*   But here's the joy; my friend and I are one;*
*   Sweet flattery! then she loves but me alone.*

41 A Naughty Blot on your Copybook

You play your naughty tricks, now and again,
if I'm not in your thoughts and in your mind:
your youth and looks attract; and in your train
always an opportunity you'll find.
A social catch, worth winning, and soon won,
a stunning sight worth going for: that's you;
and if a woman woos, what woman's son
turns his back sourly, spurns that victor too?
Oh my! But must you occupy my spot?
Couldn't you scold your looks, bawl out your youth,
who riotously bring you to what's not
good, so you go and spoil a twofold truth:
   my lady's, drawn to looks that simply thrill;
   yours, by traduction of, yours truly, Will.

42 My Girl and my Guy got it on. Good! Good!

You got my girl: that's partly why I'm faint:
my darling's lost, although that's far from worst.
My girl got you, and that's my big complaint,
an amorous loss that far outruns my first.
Two loving villains! But I find no guilt:
I drool about that lass, so you drool too;
on my account that lass disdains my suit,
on my account that lass consorts with you.
I lost you, but my loving loss is gain;
I lost my lass, my guy has found that loss;
my girl and guy both won, I lost both twain;
on my account both sponsor this, my cross.
   But look, what joy! My guy is I, and I
   am him: so I'm my girly's only guy.

XLIII

When most I wink, then do mine eyes best see,
For all the day they view things unrespected;
But when I sleep, in dreams they look on thee,
And darkly bright are bright in dark directed.
Then thou, whose shadow shadows doth make bright,
How would thy shadow's form form happy show
To the clear day with thy much clearer light,
When to unseeing eyes thy shade shines so!
How would, I say, mine eyes be blessed made
By looking on thee in the living day,
When in dead night thy fair imperfect shade
Through heavy sleep on sightless eyes doth stay!
    All days are nights to see till I see thee
    And nights bright days when dreams do show thee me.

XLIV

If the dull substance of my flesh were thought,
Injurious distance should not stop my way;
For then despite of space I would be brought,
From limits far remote where thou dost stay.
No matter then although my foot did stand
Upon the farthest earth removed from thee;
For nimble thought can jump both sea and land
As soon as think the place where he would be.
But ah! thought kills me that I am not thought,
To leap large lengths of miles when thou art gone,
But that so much of earth and water wrought
I must attend time's leisure with my moan,
    Receiving nought by elements so slow
    But heavy tears, badges of either's woe.

43 Visions and Visibility

Closing my lids is what sparks up my sight.
All day I look at unimportant sights;
but, nodding off, it's you: and darkly bright,
my orbs go brightly into coal-black nights.
Your shadow lights up shadows, it's so bright.
Wouldn't your shadow's form form happy show
in daylight with your own most lucid light,
if on shut lids your shadow casts a glow!
I'm asking you – how could my sight know bliss
by looking at you in broad light of day,
if in black night your ghostly shadow is
so fair, and apt on drooping lids to stay?
    Until I spot you, any day is night;
      your form looms up, and any night is bright.

44 Thought Can Fly, But I Can't

If my dull body was a puff of thought,
no spatial handicap would bar my way;
for, far away or not, I'd shimmy, brought
from distant limits to your instant stay.
So, no obstruction, if my foot should stand
on ground particularly far from you:
thought can jump turgid main and stolid land,
soon as it thinks what spot it's going to.
But ah, I'm slain by thought, for I'm no thought,
nimbly to bound a million yards across:
of this poor pair of humours I am wrought,
and sadly wait for days and months to pass.
    From sluggish lymph and mortar I obtain
      long-dragging sobs, disclosing both in pain.

XLV

The other two, slight air and purging fire,
Are both with thee, wherever I abide;
The first my thought, the other my desire,
These present-absent with swift motion slide.
For when these quicker elements are gone
In tender embassy of love to thee,
My life, being made of four, with two alone
Sinks down to death, oppress'd with melancholy;
Until life's composition be recurred
By those swift messengers return'd from thee,
Who even but now come back again, assured
Of thy fair health, recounting it to me:
   This told, I joy; but then no longer glad,
    I send them back again and straight grow sad.

XLVI

Mine eye and heart are at a mortal war
How to divide the conquest of thy sight;
Mine eye my heart thy picture's sight would bar,
My heart mine eye the freedom of that right.
My heart doth plead that thou in him dost lie,
A closet never pierced with crystal eyes;
But the defendant doth that plea deny
And says in him thy fair appearance lies.
To 'cide this title is impaneled
A quest of thoughts, all tenants to the heart
And by their verdict is determined
The clear eye's moiety and the dear heart's part:
   As thus; mine eye's due is thy outward part,
    And my heart's right thy inward love of heart.

45 Can't Do Without Light Humours

Third and fourth humours, lissom air and burning,
both hang with you, not noting my location;
third is my thought and fourth is all my churning,
now right to hand, now slipping fast off-station.
Anon this frisky pair may visit you
as soft ambassadors of adoration:
I should consist of four! With only two,
I sink down dying, victim of frustration,
until my composition is put right
by my two missing swift diplomatists
just coming back again, who saw you bright
and flourishing, and start narrating this.
    I'm full of joy: but not for long am glad;
    Go back! I cry: and straightaway grow sad.

46 Division of Rights

Two of my parts confront in mortal war:
this, my brain's window; that, my pump of blood.
Squabbling to own your sight, both try to bar
mutual claims upon this utmost good.
That part lays claim that you inhabit him,
a cupboard which admits no visual light;
this part says not at all, for it's in him
your wondrous apparition lands its flight.
My jury is a board of thoughts, all sworn,
all jurors lodging at my pump's accord:
and my inquiring board shall mark a bourn,
splitting this claimant's from that claimant's hoard.
    In short, my window gains your outward show;
    my *cardia*'s won your inward, loving glow.

**Plato's word for our most vital organ, as in 'cardiogram':
now thought of as bound up with our moods and passions.*

XLVII

Betwixt mine eye and heart a league is took,
And each doth good turns now unto the other:
When that mine eye is famish'd for a look,
Or heart in love with sighs himself doth smother,
With my love's picture then my eye doth feast
And to the painted banquet bids my heart;
Another time mine eye is my heart's guest
And in his thoughts of love doth share a part:
So, either by thy picture or my love,
Thyself away art present still with me;
For thou not farther than my thoughts canst move,
And I am still with them and they with thee;
    Or, if they sleep, thy picture in my sight
    Awakes my heart to heart's and eye's delight.

XLVIII

How careful was I, when I took my way,
Each trifle under truest bars to thrust,
That to my use it might unused stay
From hands of falsehood, in sure wards of trust!
But thou, to whom my jewels trifles are,
Most worthy comfort, now my greatest grief,
Thou, best of dearest and mine only care,
Art left the prey of every vulgar thief
Thee have I not lock'd up in any chest,
Save where thou art not, though I feel thou art,
Within the gentle closure of my breast,
From whence at pleasure thou mayst come and part;
    And even thence thou wilt be stol'n, I fear,
    For truth proves thievish for a prize so dear.

47 *Always Sharing*

Two of my parts concur: a pact is struck:
window and pump do mutual good turns.
If my brain's window's hungry for a look,
or if my loving motor sighs and burns,
my window has your portrait for its tasting,
and bids my motor try this paintwork food;
or on occasions it's my pump that's hosting,
sharing his loving thoughts, for window's good.
So by your portrait or my amity,
although far off, I hold and guard you still:
you can't outrun my thoughts' propinquity;
Will's thoughts will stay with you, and stay with Will.
 If thoughts nod off, your portrait in my sight
 dawns cordially and visually bright.

48 *If only I could put you away in my Strongbox…*

How cautious was I as I took my way!
All shiny stuff shut tight in bars I thrust,
in mint condition all my own to stay,
away from traitors' hands, in wards of trust!
But you, who turn to rubbish all my bling,
most worthy comfort, most sad pain of all,
you, most of all my darling and my king,
to any vulgar crook may victim fall.
I didn't lock you up in any box,
only my bosom, which can't hold you, no,
though I may think it holds, and softly rocks,
allowing you at will to stay or go,
 till from my bosom by a burglar sprung,
 a trusty's trophy, charming, fair, and young.

XLIX

Against that time, if ever that time come,
When I shall see thee frown on my defects,
When as thy love hath cast his utmost sum,
Call'd to that audit by advised respects;
Against that time when thou shalt strangely pass
And scarcely greet me with that sun thine eye,
When love, converted from the thing it was,
 Shall reasons find of settled gravity,--
Against that time do I ensconce me here
Within the knowledge of mine own desert,
 And this my hand against myself uprear,
To guard the lawful reasons on thy part:
    To leave poor me thou hast the strength of laws,
    Since why to love I can allege no cause.

L

How heavy do I journey on the way,
When what I seek, my weary travel's end,
Doth teach that ease and that repose to say
'Thus far the miles are measured from thy friend!'
The beast that bears me, tired with my woe,
Plods dully on, to bear that weight in me,
As if by some instinct the wretch did know
His rider loved not speed, being made from thee:
The bloody spur cannot provoke him on
That sometimes anger thrusts into his hide;
Which heavily he answers with a groan,
More sharp to me than spurring to his side;
    For that same groan doth put this in my mind;
    My grief lies onward and my joy behind.

49 *You may stop loving: if so,*
   I can only support you.

Against that day, supposing it rolls round,
I spot you frowning at my bad, bad points;
on which your loving, by dull duty bound,
at last adds up and audits its accounts;
against that day that you pass blankly by
and hardly nod, nor wink your optic sun,
and loving lacks its quondam quality,
turns dim and staid, and turns away from fun;
against that day I'm taking up my stand,
on guard and conscious of what I can claim:
against my own gain's good I lift my hand,
uphold your lawful right, for that's my aim.
   Abandoning poor Will's your lawful right:
   I cannot think of grounds for holding tight.

50 *Going Away from You is a Pain*

I grimly go my most laborious way,
knowing my aim, my locomotion's goal,
instructs my hour of dossing down to say
'Look at you now, far distant from your pal.'
My pain's a big load for this animal
I'm riding: downcast, plodding on so dully,
poor thing, as if with an instinctual
grasp, that away from you I'm loth to hurry.
Though I draw blood, I cannot spur him on,
angrily thrusting through his loins and flanking,
by which I just obtain a mighty groan,
that stabs my soul, his minor pain outranking.
   That groan sticks in my mind, that pain sticks fast:
   in front's my sorrow: all my joy is past.

LI

Thus can my love excuse the slow offence
Of my dull bearer when from thee I speed:
From where thou art why should I haste me thence?
Till I return, of posting is no need.
O, what excuse will my poor beast then find,
When swift extremity can seem but slow?
Then should I spur, though mounted on the wind;
In winged speed no motion shall I know:
Then can no horse with my desire keep pace;
Therefore desire of perfect'st love being made,
Shall neigh--no dull flesh--in his fiery race;
But love, for love, thus shall excuse my jade;
   Since from thee going he went wilful-slow,
   Towards thee I'll run, and give him leave to go.

LII

So am I as the rich, whose blessed key
Can bring him to his sweet up-locked treasure,
The which he will not every hour survey,
For blunting the fine point of seldom pleasure.
Therefore are feasts so solemn and so rare,
Since, seldom coming, in the long year set,
Like stones of worth they thinly placed are,
Or captain jewels in the carcanet.
So is the time that keeps you as my chest,
Or as the wardrobe which the robe doth hide,
To make some special instant special blest,
By new unfolding his imprison'd pride.
   Blessed are you, whose worthiness gives scope,
   Being had, to triumph, being lack'd, to hope.

51 My Pony is Slow. OK for Going, Not for Coming Back!

Loving you, I can pardon my slow dray,
my dimwit transport, as I part from you:
In quitting you, why would I whiz away?
Coming back, hurrying's what I must do:
and oh! what pardon will my poor nag find,
its max-fast-forward looking simply slow?
Though I might spur, on wings of rushing wind,
post-hasting: any sign of motion? No.
No racing colt can match my swift adoring.
Just watch adoring, born of total loving,
whinny, its lightning limbs in bright flight soaring!
And, loving, I'll shrug off my mount's poor moving:
    in quitting you, my mount was wilful-slow;
    I'll run back, having told it: thank you, no.

52 Your Visits Unlock My Box.

Think of a rich man with a lucky lock,
unlocking it to find that hoard of his,
but not at two and four and six o'clock,
blunting too soon his tingling points of bliss:
that's why a Christmas or Bank Holiday,
ruby or diamond, is occasional,
unusual, not too quickly on its way,
but far apart, sown thinly, if at all.
Waiting for you is similar: I lock
my cupboard, which contains my party gown,
imprisoning its glory till my clock
says I can put it on and go to town.
    Good on you! What a star! Big span of doubt:
    I triumph with you, and I wish without.

LIII

What is your substance, whereof are you made,
That millions of strange shadows on you tend?
Since every one hath, every one, one shade,
And you, but one, can every shadow lend.
Describe Adonis, and the counterfeit
Is poorly imitated after you;
On Helen's cheek all art of beauty set,
And you in Grecian tires are painted new:
Speak of the spring and foison of the year;
The one doth shadow of your beauty show,
The other as your bounty doth appear;
And you in every blessed shape we know.
　In all external grace you have some part,
　But you like none, none you, for constant heart.

LIV

O, how much more doth beauty beauteous seem
By that sweet ornament which truth doth give!
The rose looks fair, but fairer we it deem
For that sweet odour which doth in it live.
The canker-blooms have full as deep a dye
As the perfumed tincture of the roses,
Hang on such thorns and play as wantonly
When summer's breath their masked buds discloses:
But, for their virtue only is their show,
They live unwoo'd and unrespected fade,
Die to themselves. Sweet roses do not so;
Of their sweet deaths are sweetest odours made:
　And so of you, beauteous and lovely youth,
　When that shall fade, my verse distills your truth.

53 So Many Shadows, and You...

What sort of stuff do you consist of? Ooh,
millions of curious shadows hang around:
for nothing has two shadows, nor do you:
but you can furnish shadows to astound.
Portray Adonis, and his photofit
is a poor imitation, drawn from you;
Paris of Troy, his woman's out of it:
that paintwork's yours, it's your Corinthian do.
Talk about spring, and talk of autumn's fall:
spring shows your form in shadow, whilst anon
autumn's your bounty, ours to know in all
your glorious forms, fair fruits in shining sun.
    You stand with any outward show, fair youth,
    But nobody can match your loyal truth.

54 A Horticultural Analogy: It's Not Just Looks

You'd add so much on top of your good looks
by adding truth, a fitting final touch!
A Tudor bloom looks good, but in our books
its fragrant odour counts for just as much.
Rosa canina's just as colourful
as its most aromatic courtly kin:
hangs too on briars, plays just as fanciful
tricks with its darling buds, as May blows in.
Alas! It's only good for visual show:
sought out by nobody, it wilts unsung,
dying in purdah. Tudors' odours blow,
fragrantly fading: potpourris, not dung.
    So too for you, you bootylicious youth:
    you'll wilt; Will's stanzas will distil your truth.

LV

Not marble, nor the gilded monuments
Of princes, shall outlive this powerful rhyme;
But you shall shine more bright in these contents
Than unswept stone besmear'd with sluttish time.
When wasteful war shall statues overturn
And broils root out the work of masonry,
Nor Mars his sword nor war's quick fire shall burn
The living record of your memory.
'Gainst death and all-oblivious enmity
Shall you pace forth; your praise shall still find room
Even in the eyes of all posterity
That wear this world out to the ending doom.
    So, till the judgment that yourself arise,
    You live in this, and dwell in lover's eyes.

LVI

Sweet love, renew thy force; be it not said
Thy edge should blunter be than appetite,
Which but to-day by feeding is allay'd,
To-morrow sharpen'd in his former might:
So, love, be thou; although to-day thou fill
Thy hungry eyes even till they wink with fullness,
To-morrow see again, and do not kill
The spirit of love with a perpetual dullness.
Let this sad interim like the ocean be
Which parts the shore, where two contracted new
Come daily to the banks, that, when they see
Return of love, more blest may be the view;
    Else call it winter, which being full of care
    Makes summer's welcome thrice more wish'd, more rare.

55 *Parian Masonry Won't Outlast This Book*

Not Parian masonry nor royalty's
gilt pillars shall outlast my puissant writing.
I'll burnish you! That wilting glory is
soon spoilt with dirt and stains and drab days' blighting.
Wars uproot statuary from our map;
conflicts disrupt big buildings' workmanship;
not Mars's sword nor flash of war can zap
and burn this book, your long-surviving scrip.
Against oblivion's hostility,
against annihilation, you'll find room,
room to tough out uncouth futurity,
which frowns at all of us till final doom.
    So, till you stir on Doomsday, know that my
    fond looks shall guard you, and this prosody.

56 *Full up? I want you hungry again!*

Darling, look sharp, man up! - for folk might say
you cut as blunt as that voracity
which was run down by victualling today:
tomorrow, sharp at full capacity.
Darling, do that: although today you fill
your starving optic till it shuts, chock full,
tomorrow look again, and do not kill
that loving spirit: don't stay stuck on Dull!
Our dismal gap is as the bounding main
that parts two coasts, and a contractual pair
stands daily on its banks, to scan again
a darling's form, a sight that's passing fair.
    So months of cold, worn down with pain and sorrow,
    long for warm days and hail a bright tomorrow.

LVII

Being your slave, what should I do but tend
Upon the hours and times of your desire?
I have no precious time at all to spend,
Nor services to do, till you require.
Nor dare I chide the world-without-end hour
Whilst I, my sovereign, watch the clock for you,
Nor think the bitterness of absence sour
When you have bid your servant once adieu;
Nor dare I question with my jealous thought
Where you may be, or your affairs suppose,
But, like a sad slave, stay and think of nought
Save, where you are how happy you make those.
   So true a fool is love that in your will,
   Though you do any thing, he thinks no ill.

LVIII

That god forbid that made me first your slave,
I should in thought control your times of pleasure,
Or at your hand the account of hours to crave,
Being your vassal, bound to stay your leisure!
O, let me suffer, being at your beck,
The imprison'd absence of your liberty;
And patience, tame to sufferance, bide each check,
Without accusing you of injury.
Be where you list, your charter is so strong
That you yourself may privilege your time
To what you will; to you it doth belong
Yourself to pardon of self-doing crime.
   I am to wait, though waiting so be hell;
   Not blame your pleasure, be it ill or well.

57 *I am your Dogsbody, your Doormat.*

I am your dogsbody. What must I do?
Wait on all hours and timings of your whim.
Can't simply shirk, do my own missions. You
call all my shots. No jobs, but what's 'for him'.
To scold infinity's long-drawn-out hour?
No, mighty king! for I must watch your clock;
no right to think of parting's pain as sour,
if you dismiss your Will, your Jovial Jock;
no right to ask with my invidious thought
in what location your affairs unfold;
sad dogsbody, I stay and think of nought
but you: with whom you sport, what jaunts you hold.
    Amour is such an ass, that in your will,
    anything you may do, 'tis thought no ill.

58 *I can't control what you do...*
I must put up with it.

That god forbid, by whom I'm put in thrall
that I'd in thought control your hours of wassail,
ask you in writing to account for all:
I'm bound to stand and wait, for I'm your vassal.
Grant, in my toil, I may hold on, put up
with you far off, and my captivity:
grant I stay mild, withstanding any stop,
without accusing you of injury.
In all locations your authority
allows you anything you wish to do:
that is your right and your immunity;
you grant your own wrongdoings' pardon, too.
    And I must wait, though that is agonising,
    for good or ill, your whim not criticising.

LIX

If there be nothing new, but that which is
Hath been before, how are our brains beguiled,
Which, labouring for invention, bear amiss
The second burden of a former child!
O, that record could with a backward look,
Even of five hundred courses of the sun,
Show me your image in some antique book,
Since mind at first in character was done!
That I might see what the old world could say
To this composed wonder of your frame;
Whether we are mended, or whether better they,
Or whether revolution be the same.
    O, sure I am, the wits of former days
    To subjects worse have given admiring praise.

LX

Like as the waves make towards the pebbled shore,
So do our minutes hasten to their end;
Each changing place with that which goes before,
In sequent toil all forwards do contend.
Nativity, once in the main of light,
Crawls to maturity, wherewith being crown'd,
Crooked eclipses 'gainst his glory fight,
And Time that gave doth now his gift confound.
Time doth transfix the flourish set on youth
And delves the parallels in beauty's brow,
Feeds on the rarities of nature's truth,
And nothing stands but for his scythe to mow:
    And yet to times in hope my verse shall stand,
    Praising thy worth, despite his cruel hand.

59 *If I Could Look Back In History...*

If all that is, is not innovatory,
if all is old: how baffling for our brain,
to try for what's unknown, and to miscarry
with child laboriously born again.
Could but a DVD, with backward look
at half a thousand rounds of circling sun,
display your portrait in a fusty book,
your spirit and your look both truly won:
so I might know what that old world could say
of you, you most amazing composition.
Can history stand up against today?
Is no gain found by cyclical addition?
    Without a doubt, pundits in past days would
    lavish hurrahs on guys not half as good.

60 *Victims of Chronology; Survival of my Stanzas*

Surf runs and rolls towards a stony strand;
our hours and days rush onward, bound for doom.
What follows soon has front position, and
anon a third. Bustling continuum!
Nativity (that's Birth) bursts into light,
crawls to maturity and sports its crown,
till untoward obstructions quash such sight:
clocks twirl, and build it up, and knock it down,
twirl and transfix that flourishing of youth
and dig stark furrows in a glorious brow,
gnawing on natural outstanding truth
till nothing stands for falchion's sharp to mow.
    But no! My stanzas optimistic stand,
    praising your worth, to flout that horrid hand.

LXI

Is it thy will thy image should keep open
My heavy eyelids to the weary night?
Dost thou desire my slumbers should be broken,
While shadows like to thee do mock my sight?
Is it thy spirit that thou send'st from thee
So far from home into my deeds to pry,
To find out shames and idle hours in me,
The scope and tenor of thy jealousy?
O, no! thy love, though much, is not so great:
It is my love that keeps mine eye awake;
Mine own true love that doth my rest defeat,
To play the watchman ever for thy sake:
    For thee watch I whilst thou dost wake elsewhere,
    From me far off, with others all too near.

LXII

Sin of self-love possesseth all mine eye
And all my soul and all my every part;
And for this sin there is no remedy,
It is so grounded inward in my heart.
Methinks no face so gracious is as mine,
No shape so true, no truth of such account;
And for myself mine own worth do define,
As I all other in all worths surmount.
But when my glass shows me myself indeed,
Beated and chopp'd with tann'd antiquity,
Mine own self-love quite contrary I read;
Self so self-loving were iniquity.
    'Tis thee, myself, that for myself I praise,
    Painting my age with beauty of thy days.

61 *I Can't Drop Off, for Visions of You*

Is it your will your portrait should prop up
my drowsy lids to look at laggard night?
Should I, insomniac, with ghosts sit up,
shadows, who took your looks to mock my sight?
Is your familiar on long warranty
to pry into my doings? Your ambition,
to bring to light my sloth and infamy?
Stands this as cut and thrust of your suspicion?
O no! Your loving stops far short of raving:
it is my loving holds my lids from closing.
I play night-watchman always, for your saving:
my own addiction thwarts my tranquil dozing.
    For you I stay on watch, far from your waking,
    and far from all who stand round you, partaking.

62 *Am I narcissistic? It's all about You.*

A sinful autophilia grips my I,
my orb and all my soul, my front, my back;
and for this sin no balsam can apply:
it's sunk right down into my cardiac.
I think no phiz as gracious as my own,
no form so right, no fact of such account,
and on my own I pin my own worth down:
all also-rans in all worths I surmount.
But oh! my mirror's showing fact, not fiction:
I'm worn and torn with brown antiquity!
My autophilia's in contradiction,
now autophilia's rank iniquity.
    It's you I laud, my soul: my long old tooth
    I paint with colours of your glorious youth.

LXIII

Against my love shall be, as I am now,
With Time's injurious hand crush'd and o'er-worn;
When hours have drain'd his blood and fill'd his brow
With lines and wrinkles; when his youthful morn
Hath travell'd on to ag"'s steepy night,
And all those beauties whereof now he's king
Are vanishing or vanish'd out of sight,
Stealing away the treasure of his spring;
For such a time do I now fortify
Against confounding age's cruel knife,
That he shall never cut from memory
My sweet love's beauty, though my lover's life:
   His beauty shall in these black lines be seen,
   And they shall live, and he in them still green.

LXIV

When I have seen by Time's fell hand defaced
The rich proud cost of outworn buried age;
When sometime lofty towers I see down-razed
And brass eternal slave to mortal rage;
When I have seen the hungry ocean gain
Advantage on the kingdom of the shore,
And the firm soil win of the watery main,
Increasing store with loss and loss with store;
When I have seen such interchange of state,
Or state itself confounded to decay;
Ruin hath taught me thus to ruminate,
That Time will come and take my love away.
   This thought is as a death, which cannot choose
   But weep to have that which it fears to lose.

63 My Darling will Grow Old:
I Guard his Glory by Writing!

Too soon, my chuck will stand as I do now,
by Timing's horrid hand brought down, outworn;
for Hours shall drain his blood and fill his brow
with scrawls and furrows, and his youthful morn
shall pass along to old man's arduous night;
that blazing radiant bloom that crowns him king
is vanishing, has slunk off out of sight,
purloining all that dowry of his spring.
Against that day I now shall fortify,
against confounding Anno Domini,
who shall not slash and cut injuriously
my vision of fair form, though soul shall fly.
    That vision still my inky scrawls shall show,
    by which surviving, go my darling, go!

64 Anguish about Mutability and Mortality

How fifty thousand months rough up and wound
what's now a ruin, rich in days outworn!
How a high building is brought low to ground,
and rustproof brass bows down to mortal scorn!
A hungry flood gains ground, and this I saw,
crashing against our kingdom's coastal rim;
firm soil may follow a contrary law,
balancing loss and gain of tilth and swim.
I saw this mutual mutability
of status; and how long shall status stay?
By ruins I'm taught to think I must stand by
until at last my darling's took away.
    Such thought is tantamount to *thanatos*:
    in pain, I hold you: I'm afraid of loss.

*Tags: Mors, mortis; Charon, Styx, Dis, Pluto;
Clotho, Atropos; Aiakos, Minos, Rhadamanthos.*

LXV

Since brass, nor stone, nor earth, nor boundless sea,
But sad mortality o'er-sways their power,
How with this rage shall beauty hold a plea,
Whose action is no stronger than a flower?
O, how shall summer's honey breath hold out
Against the wreckful siege of battering days,
When rocks impregnable are not so stout,
Nor gates of steel so strong, but Time decays?
O fearful meditation! where, alack,
Shall Time's best jewel from Time's chest lie hid?
Or what strong hand can hold his swift foot back?
Or who his spoil of beauty can forbid?
   O, none, unless this miracle have might,
   That in black ink my love may still shine bright.

LXVI

Tired with all these, for restful death I cry,
As, to behold desert a beggar born,
And needy nothing trimm'd in jollity,
And purest faith unhappily forsworn,
And gilded honour shamefully misplaced,
And maiden virtue rudely strumpeted,
And right perfection wrongfully disgraced,
And strength by limping sway disabled,
And art made tongue-tied by authority,
And folly, doctor-like, controlling skill,
And simple truth miscall'd simplicity,
And captive good attending captain ill:
   Tired with all these, from these would I be gone,
   Save that, to die, I leave my love alone.

65 What can stop your gradual dissolution? My Stanzas!

Not brass, not rock, not land nor far-flung flood
can hold its own 'gainst sad mortality:
so how shall pulchritudo's blurt hold good
against such wrath? A bloom's fragility!
O! how shall August's apian air hold out
against assaulting days with ruinous ramming,
if rocks of adamant stand not so stout,
nor iron portals strong, unstrung by Timing!
Horrid to think about it! How, alack,
shall you, his diamond, from his box stay hid?
Or what strong hand can hold his swift foot back?
Or who his spoliation can forbid?
   Nobody! Just this bit of magick might
   do it, that in black ink my crush glows bright.

66 Sick of it all, I'd quit, but for....

Sick of it all, I long for R.I.P....
of virtuous worth in harsh starvation born,
and good-for-nothings got up gaudily,
and shining faith unhappily forsworn,
and gold-wrought honour scandalously lost,
and virgin chastity that prinks a pimp,
and rightful glory wrongfully miscast,
and vigour put at nought by lurching limp,
and art struck dumb by rough authority,
and folly's know-all fraud controlling skill,
and plain truth shown as plain stupidity,
and good in chains to wait on captain ill:
   sick of it all, I hark to Charon's calling:
   but dying is abandoning my darling.

LXVII

Ah! wherefore with infection should he live,
And with his presence grace impiety,
That sin by him advantage should achieve
And lace itself with his society?
Why should false painting imitate his cheek
And steal dead seeing of his living hue?
Why should poor beauty indirectly seek
Roses of shadow, since his rose is true?
Why should he live, now Nature bankrupt is,
Beggar'd of blood to blush through lively veins?
For she hath no exchequer now but his,
And, proud of many, lives upon his gains.
   O, him she stores, to show what wealth she had
   In days long since, before these last so bad.

LXVIII

Thus is his cheek the map of days outworn,
When beauty lived and died as flowers do now,
Before the bastard signs of fair were born,
Or durst inhabit on a living brow;
Before the golden tresses of the dead,
The right of sepulchres, were shorn away,
To live a second life on second head,
Ere beauty's dead fleece made another gay:
In him those holy antique hours are seen,
Without all ornament, itself and true,
Making no summer of another's green,
Robbing no old to dress his beauty new;
   And him as for a map doth Nature store,
   To show false Art what beauty was of yore.

67 *Why should this youth pay for a natural Bankruptcy?*

Why should this youth, amid our world's wrongdoing,
dignify sin by his proximity?
So sin draws profit out of him, accruing
by frills and thrills of his sodality.
Why should trick paintwork track his facial bloom,
filch a stiff copy of his living tint?
Why should poor glamour want a bloom of gloom,
of shadow? Is his own about to stint?
Natura's bankrupt now. Why should a loan
of all his blood unblush his limbs and brains?
No bloodbank now is drawn on but his own,
that bankrolls natural glory by his gains.
    Natura hoards him, shows what luck was had
    in days of long ago, not half so bad.

68 *His Physiognomy is of a Most Original Quality.*

His phiz! - a map of days now long outworn:
good looks did wax and wilt as blooms do now,
nor any bastard sign of fair was born,
nor durst inhabit on a living brow;
nor was gold hair, which fatal Norn struck down,
birthright of tombs, uncouthly shorn away,
living again on loan to loaning crown,
a wig brought back from Styx, a topknot gay.
In him such holy hours of long ago
show through, a *Ding an sich* with no adorning,
not hiring vigour for his May-months, no,
not robbing old to mould a glorious morning,
    This lad's a roadmap Truth shall hoard apart,
    our Old Gold Standard, shown to knavish Art.

Ding an sich: Thing as such.
Not as strict a translation as it looks.

LXIX

Those parts of thee that the world's eye doth view
Want nothing that the thought of hearts can mend;
All tongues, the voice of souls, give thee that due,
Uttering bare truth, even so as foes commend.
Thy outward thus with outward praise is crown'd;
But those same tongues that give thee so thine own
In other accents do this praise confound
By seeing farther than the eye hath shown.
They look into the beauty of thy mind,
And that, in guess, they measure by thy deeds;
Then, churls, their thoughts, although their eyes were kind,
To thy fair flower add the rank smell of weeds:
    But why thy odour matcheth not thy show,
    The soil is this, that thou dost common grow.

LXX

That thou art blamed shall not be thy defect,
For slander's mark was ever yet the fair;
The ornament of beauty is suspect,
A crow that flies in heaven's sweetest air.
So thou be good, slander doth but approve
Thy worth the greater, being woo'd of time;
For canker vice the sweetest buds doth love,
And thou present'st a pure unstained prime.
Thou hast pass'd by the ambush of young days,
Either not assail'd or victor being charged;
Yet this thy praise cannot be so thy praise,
To tie up envy evermore enlarged:
    If some suspect of ill mask'd not thy show,
    Then thou alone kingdoms of hearts shouldst owe.

69 *You look good but what you do is malodorous.*

Such parts of you as anybody scans
lack nothing that our cordial thoughts can fix;
any soul's quackbox, any larynx, plans
to honour you with straight honorifics,
saying stark truths that dastards too propound.
Ah, but that quackbox, giving you your own
honours, will mix in stuff that will confound,
by probing what no ocular has shown.
It runs a valuation of your mind -
and how fair's that? - judging by what you do;
its churlish thought, although its look was kind,
adds to your glorious bloom a rank poo-poo.
    Why can't your odour match your dazzling show?
    I'll dish your dirt. Common! That's how you grow.

70 *All this calumny just confirms your high worth*

Brickbats assail you. Not through your omission:
calumny always hits a hunky guy.
What would accompany good looks? Suspicion,
a crow aloft in any glorious sky!
If you do good, bad mouths will only show
your lasting worth, confirming you top-notch;
it's for top buds that nasty blight will go,
and you put forward youth without a blotch.
Avoiding any ambush of young days,
you fought no fight, or possibly you won;
you won your bays; but I don't think your bays
can stop th' invidious, always prowling on.
    Did no suspicion cloud your shining show,
    you'd own all amorous kingdoms. Gigolo!

LXXI

No longer mourn for me when I am dead
Than you shall hear the surly sullen bell
Give warning to the world that I am fled
From this vile world, with vilest worms to dwell:
Nay, if you read this line, remember not
The hand that writ it; for I love you so
That I in your sweet thoughts would be forgot
If thinking on me then should make you woe.
O, if, I say, you look upon this verse
When I perhaps compounded am with clay,
Do not so much as my poor name rehearse.
But let your love even with my life decay,
 Lest the wise world should look into your moan
 And mock you with me after I am gone.

LXXII

O, lest the world should task you to recite
What merit lived in me, that you should love
After my death, dear love, forget me quite,
For you in me can nothing worthy prove;
Unless you would devise some virtuous lie,
To do more for me than mine own desert,
And hang more praise upon deceased I
Than niggard truth would willingly impart:
 O, lest your true love may seem false in this,
That you for love speak well of me untrue,
My name be buried where my body is,
And live no more to shame nor me nor you.
 For I am shamed by that which I bring forth,
 And so should you, to love things nothing worth.

71 Don't mourn my parting, if it hurts to do so.

Don't mourn my shuffling off this mortal spiral
for long: quit soon as my sad tolling fails,
which warns that I'm not with us, torn from viral
low world to viral worms, low animals.
Nay, if you scan this stanza, pray do not
think about what hand writ it: loving so,
from your soft thoughts I want to slip forgot,
if it's a pain to think on your old jo.
O! if, I say, you look upon this ditty,
and I, no doubt, am in a clod of clay,
just do not say my monica, for pity,
which, with your loving, ought to slip away.
    For worldly wits would look into your moan,
    on my account to mock you, on your own.

Monica (sic): *strictly, an alias, not a normal nominal;
of doubtful origin: possibly* monkish *on taking vows.*

72 Don't try to pump up my status posthumously.

My worry: folk may task you to unwind
what was so good about your jo, that you
should cling still at my tomb. So, void your mind,
for nothing's good that you can say, or do.
You only might concoct a virtuous porky,
outstripping my poor story by your art,
outpraising all, to to primp my shadow murky,
that tightwad truth would willingly impart.
You risk your loving looking dubious,
if you for loving loudly trump untruth.
Bury my status in my tumulus:
living, it brings dishonour on us both.
    For my dishonour's that which I bring forth,
    and yours is loving what is nothing worth.

Porky: London rhyming slang for untruth.

LXXIII

That time of year thou mayst in me behold
When yellow leaves, or none, or few, do hang
Upon those boughs which shake against the cold,
Bare ruin'd choirs, where late the sweet birds sang.
In me thou seest the twilight of such day
As after sunset fadeth in the west,
Which by and by black night doth take away,
Death's second self, that seals up all in rest.
In me thou see'st the glowing of such fire
That on the ashes of his youth doth lie,
As the death-bed whereon it must expire
Consumed with that which it was nourish'd by.
   This thou perceivest, which makes thy love more strong,
   To love that well which thou must leave ere long.

LXIV

But be contented: when that fell arrest
Without all bail shall carry me away,
My life hath in this line some interest,
Which for memorial still with thee shall stay.
When thou reviewest this, thou dost review
The very part was consecrate to thee:
The earth can have but earth, which is his due;
My spirit is thine, the better part of me:
So then thou hast but lost the dregs of life,
The prey of worms, my body being dead,
The coward conquest of a wretch's knife,
Too base of thee to be remembered.
   The worth of that is that which it contains,
   And that is this, and this with thee remains.

73 *I Am Old.*

I'm in my autumn, if you'll kindly look,
with hardly any fading scraps to hang
about my boughs, kirkstalls that chill winds shook,
ruinous rotting choirs in which birds sang.
I am a twilight of a dying day,
As sunlight drowns its dusky orison,
which by and by black night conducts away,
sibling of doom, who grants oblivion.
I am a burnt-out brand that's still aglow,
lying on cold ash of my long-lost youth,
moribund, all forlorn, about to go,
bit by my quondam food, with callous tooth.
   You spot this fact: your passion still is strong:
   you know I won't hang out with you for long.

74 *My body will pass away, but not my soul, not my words.*

Just do not worry if a hand distrains,
without all bail, to carry Will away:
a fair accrual still my work sustains,
which as a talisman with you shall stay.
You'll look at this, you'll look at what I paid,
put out for you, a sacral gift, today:
in lowly dust my dust is duly laid,
my spirit's yours, and that's what soars away.
What you will count as lost is worldly trash,
foodstuff for worms, my body laid in ground:
poor victim of a dismal coward slash,
not fit for you to wrap your thoughts around.
   That husk outworn its inward worth displays,
   and that is this, abiding, yours always.

LXXV

So are you to my thoughts as food to life,
 Or as sweet-season'd showers are to the ground;
And for the peace of you I hold such strife
As 'twixt a miser and his wealth is found;
Now proud as an enjoyer and anon
Doubting the filching age will steal his treasure,
Now counting best to be with you alone,
Then better'd that the world may see my pleasure;
Sometime all full with feasting on your sight
And by and by clean starved for a look;
Possessing or pursuing no delight,
Save what is had or must from you be took.
   Thus do I pine and surfeit day by day,
   Or gluttoning on all, or all away.

LXXVI

Why is my verse so barren of new pride,
So far from variation or quick change?
Why with the time do I not glance aside
To new-found methods and to compounds strange?
Why write I still all one, ever the same,
And keep invention in a noted weed,
That every word doth almost tell my name,
Showing their birth and where they did proceed?
O, know, sweet love, I always write of you,
And you and love are still my argument;
So all my best is dressing old words new,
Spending again what is already spent:
   For as the sun is daily new and old,
   So is my love still telling what is told.

75 I'm Rich or Poor, Gorging or Starving

So art thou to my thoughts as food to living,
or cloudburst's fragrant rainfall to dry ground;
and for your calm of mind I hold such striving
as 'twixt *Old Goriot and his hoard was found:
now proud in usufruct, now in dark mood,
anxious this filching world may rob him blind:
now counting privacy my utmost good,
now, passing utmost, flaunting to mankind;
now all full up with gorging on your sight,
and by and by just starving for a look.
Joy's flown: I hold, who could not halt its flight,
just what I had from you, or what I took.
 Now I'm a pig, now hungry, day by day,
  now gluttoning on all, now all away.

Balzac's notorious tightwad.

76 It's my old topic, my only topic!

Why is my writing short of innovation?
Why don't I look for only-just-found ways?
Why no quick nip-and-tuck, no variation,
no fancy compounds, to adorn my lays?
Why am I writing still immutably,
clothing my hard-won thoughts in outworn drag,
so any word proclaims (or almost) my
monica, shows its birth and flaunts my flag?
You know, my chuck, my topic's always you,
my Cupid, intransmutably broadcast:
old words brought back, that's all that I can do,
passing again what long ago was past.
 As sunlight daily is both born and old,
  my loving simply parrots what was told.

LXXVII

Thy glass will show thee how thy beauties wear,
Thy dial how thy precious minutes waste;
The vacant leaves thy mind's imprint will bear,
And of this book this learning mayst thou taste.
The wrinkles which thy glass will truly show
Of mouthed graves will give thee memory;
Thou by thy dial's shady stealth mayst know
Time's thievish progress to eternity.
Look, what thy memory can not contain
 Commit to these waste blanks, and thou shalt find
Those children nursed, deliver'd from thy brain,
To take a new acquaintance of thy mind.
    These offices, so oft as thou wilt look,
    Shall profit thee and much enrich thy book.

LXXVIII

So oft have I invoked thee for my Muse
And found such fair assistance in my verse
As every alien pen hath got my use
And under thee their poesy disperse.
Thine eyes that taught the dumb on high to sing
And heavy ignorance aloft to fly
Have added feathers to the learned's wing
And given grace a double majesty.
Yet be most proud of that which I compile,
Whose influence is thine and born of thee:
In others' works thou dost but mend the style,
And arts with thy sweet graces graced be;
    But thou art all my art and dost advance
    As high as learning my rude ignorance.

77 Mirror and Clock...
you'll fill in what I didn't say.

Your glass will show you how your good looks last,
your clock-dial how your vital hours run past;
gaps in my book will carry your mind's cast;
you'll know what's taught by this, my book, at last!
Such furrows as your glass will truly show
will call to mind a ditch that's six foot long;
your clock will mark burglarious hours in slow
march to infinity, that do us wrong.
Look what your cranium cannot contain,
commit it to my gaps, and you shall find
plump nursling infants, offspring of your brain,
coming and taking station in your mind.
    Thanks to such functions, any day you look,
    you'll profit, with rich pickings from your book.

78 In Anon's Work Thou Art Marginal,
In My Work Pivotal.

Oft as I call on you for inspiration,
finding such top-notch succour in my toil:
so now Anon starts scribbling in my station,
spilling about your foot his bardic spoil.
Your iris taught dumb souls on high to sing
and ignoramus clods aloft to fly:
put a strong pinion on a scholar's wing,
brought twofold honour to nobility.
But first flaunt this, my book which I amass:
its gist is yours, its origin is you;
in Anon's works you add a touch of class,
light gracing of his art, that's all you do;
    but thou art all my art, promoting high,
    as high as scholarship, my bumpkinry.

'Anon': a rival wordsmith: possibly, too, a rival suitor.

LXXIX

Whilst I alone did call upon thy aid,
My verse alone had all thy gentle grace,
But now my gracious numbers are decay'd
And my sick Muse doth give another place.
I grant, sweet love, thy lovely argument
Deserves the travail of a worthier pen,
Yet what of thee thy poet doth invent
He robs thee of and pays it thee again.
He lends thee virtue and he stole that word
From thy behaviour; beauty doth he give
And found it in thy cheek; he can afford
No praise to thee but what in thee doth live.
   Then thank him not for that which he doth say,
   Since what he owes thee thou thyself dost pay.

LXXX

O, how I faint when I of you do write,
Knowing a better spirit doth use your name,
And in the praise thereof spends all his might,
To make me tongue-tied, speaking of your fame!
But since your worth, wide as the ocean is,
The humble as the proudest sail doth bear,
My saucy bark inferior far to his
On your broad main doth willfully appear.
Your shallowest help will hold me up afloat,
Whilst he upon your soundless deep doth ride;
Or being wreck'd, I am a worthless boat,
He of tall building and of goodly pride:
   Then if he thrive and I be cast away,
   The worst was this; my love was my decay.

79 *That rival bard purloins all your good points.*

Whilst only I was asking for your aid,
only my stanzas won your kind approval;
but now my skill's worn out, and I'm afraid
my sickly inspiration has a rival!
I grant, my darling, that your thrilling script
ought not to flow from my too middling quill;
but anything yon wordsmith may concoct
is burglary from you, paid back in full.
Calling you virtuous! It's yours, that word,
spun from your conduct. Calls you bonny – took
that word straight off your phiz; and can accord
you no good word that isn't in your book.
    Don't thank Anon for what Anon will say:
    Anon should pay you court: it's you who pay.

80 *A Nautical Stand-Off*

Oh how I faint as I of you indict,
knowing that by my rival I'm outrun,
who puffs your glory up with all his might:
my throat's a tight-knit knot, it isn't fun.
But your vast glory is a flood flung far,
on which both lowly ships and proud can sail:
my saucy fishing-smack's no man-of-war,
but I go bobbing in his vapour-trail.
Among your shoals and shallows I can float
and watch him draw full fathoms on your main;
or I may sink, a most unworthy boat,
incurring his top-gallant's high disdain.
    Worst, grant him luck, and I'm a castaway:
    and it's by loving that I go astray.

LXXXI

Or I shall live your epitaph to make,
Or you survive when I in earth am rotten;
From hence your memory death cannot take,
Although in me each part will be forgotten.
Your name from hence immortal life shall have,
Though I, once gone, to all the world must die:
The earth can yield me but a common grave,
When you entombed in men's eyes shall lie.
Your monument shall be my gentle verse,
Which eyes not yet created shall o'er-read,
And tongues to be your being shall rehearse
When all the breathers of this world are dead;
 You still shall live--such virtue hath my pen--
 Where breath most breathes, even in the mouths of men.

LXXXII

I grant thou wert not married to my Muse
And therefore mayst without attaint o'erlook
The dedicated words which writers use
Of their fair subject, blessing every book.
Thou art as fair in knowledge as in hue,
Finding thy worth a limit past my praise,
And therefore art enforced to seek anew
Some fresher stamp of the time-bettering days.
And do so, love; yet when they have devised
What strained touches rhetoric can lend,
Thou truly fair wert truly sympathized
In true plain words by thy true-telling friend;
 And their gross painting might be better used
 Where cheeks need blood; in thee it is abused.

81 Which of us will Go First? Your Immortality

Options: I'll sculpt your tomb's obituary,
or you will last, surviving as I rot.
Mortality can't filch your obvious glory,
but all my lock and stock must fall forgot;
from this point on your monica's undying,
but I'll turn cold, this mortal world I'll quit:
in common tomb of soil I'm fit for lying;
your glory, though, for sight of all is fit.
You'll mark your tomb with my kind prosody,
a mark for scanning by bright brains unborn;
and lips unborn shall hymn your quality,
though all who now draw air shall fall forlorn.
    On human lips, thanks to my virtuous quill,
    in roads of air you'll stay, surviving still.

82 My Portrayal of you is truthful; Anon's isn't.

I grant you didn't marry my Parnassian,
my guiding spirit: it's your right to look
at what 'Anon' or I say on occasion
about you, introducing any book.
As fair in wisdom as in colouring,
you find your worth outruns my poor ability,
and so must look around to find what thing,
what stamp will fit our fancy days' facility.
Do it, my chuck! Anon may twist and try
and strain for sophistry sophistical;
I show you, truly fair, with sympathy:
truth said in plain words by your truthful pal.
    Anon's gross painting might turn out OK
    on pallid brows, but not on you, no way.

LXXXIII

I never saw that you did painting need
And therefore to your fair no painting set;
I found, or thought I found, you did exceed
The barren tender of a poet's debt;
And therefore have I slept in your report,
That you yourself being extant well might show
How far a modern quill doth come too short,
Speaking of worth, what worth in you doth grow.
This silence for my sin you did impute,
Which shall be most my glory, being dumb;
For I impair not beauty being mute,
When others would give life and bring a tomb.
   There lives more life in one of your fair eyes
   Than both your poets can in praise devise.

LXXXIV

Who is it that says most? which can say more
Than this rich praise, that you alone are you?
In whose confine immured is the store
Which should example where your equal grew.
Lean penury within that pen doth dwell
That to his subject lends not some small glory;
But he that writes of you, if he can tell
That you are you, so dignifies his story,
Let him but copy what in you is writ,
Not making worse what nature made so clear,
And such a counterpart shall fame his wit,
Making his style admired every where.
   You to your beauteous blessings add a curse,
   Being fond on praise, which makes your praises worse.

83 *No Point in putting any Paint on You!*

Not having thought of you as short of paint,
I put no paint on bonny brilliant you.
I thought I found you out of all constraint,
past anything a bard could say or do.
I'd just nod off, not saying (as I ought)
what you, in bloom, convincingly could show:
how far a modish quill can fall too short,
talking of worth, what worth in you doth grow.
You took for sin my taciturnity,
but it's my blatant glory that I'm dumb:
that way, I don't impair your quality;
Anon, who aims at vivid, brings a tomb.
    Such vivid orbs, both L and R, of sight!
    Your pair of bards can't touch your living light.

84 *Not hard to do it. Sadly, adulation is your drug.*

Who is it that says most? What can outsay
this loving word, that only thou art thou?
What lock-up harbours data to portray
historic rivals fit to match you now?
How poor, how bankrupt is that stylus which
can't tint its topic with a touch of glory!
Writing of you, a bard has but to pitch
that thou art thou: 'twill glorify his story.
Only to copy what in you is writ,
not spoil what's naturally obvious:
such mimicry wins honour for his wit,
and admiration most ubiquitous.
    You blight your luck, fair chuck, with adulation:
    too fond of it! - and that's an aggravation.

LXXXV

My tongue-tied Muse in manners holds her still,
While comments of your praise, richly compiled,
Reserve their character with golden quill
And precious phrase by all the Muses filed.
I think good thoughts whilst other write good words,
And like unletter'd clerk still cry 'Amen'
To every hymn that able spirit affords
In polish'd form of well-refined pen.
Hearing you praised, I say ' 'Tis so, 'tis true,'
And to the most of praise add something more;
But that is in my thought, whose love to you,
Though words come hindmost, holds his rank before.
   Then others for the breath of words respect,
   Me for my dumb thoughts, speaking in effect.

LXXXVI

Was it the proud full sail of his great verse,
Bound for the prize of all too precious you,
That did my ripe thoughts in my brain inhearse,
Making their tomb the womb wherein they grew?
Was it his spirit, by spirits taught to write
Above a mortal pitch, that struck me dead?
No, neither he, nor his compeers by night
Giving him aid, my verse astonished.
He, nor that affable familiar ghost
Which nightly gulls him with intelligence
As victors of my silence cannot boast;
I was not sick of any fear from thence:
   But when your countenance fill'd up his line,
   Then lack'd I matter; that enfeebled mine.

85 *I Think Good Thoughts,*
   Anon Churns Out Good Words.

I'm stuck. No inspiration. Stuck, stock still.
Anon, though, lavishly concocts your lauds,
props up your quality with gold-tip quill,
Parnassian posh from duos, trios, quads.
I think good thoughts, Anon churns out good words:
I cry, as bumpkin church-boys do, Right On! -
praising all hymns a skilful mind affords
with polish of a *courtly dict-i-on*.
I log his words, I say 'I think so too',
and to his total puff I add a punt:
but that is in my thought, which loving you,
though words trail hindmost, holds its rank in front.
    So hail Anon for his vocabulary,
    and hail yours truly, thought's dumb luminary.

86 *My Rival Was Writing About You*

Was it in proud full sail his mighty words,
outbound to hijack oh-so-darling you,
shut all my growing thoughts in my brain's shrouds,
making that womb of growth a grim tomb too?
Was it his spirit's trick, by spirits taught
to sing past mortal pitch, that I got ill?
It wasn't him, no, nor his night-support
companions, shaking to its roots my quill:
not him, and not that frank familiar ghost
which nightly gulls him with disinformation,
could staunch my flow, and flaunt a victor's boast.
I swoon with no such discombobulation.
    But I saw you in it, and that was tough:
    you, grinning out. And I ran out of puff.

LXXXVII

Farewell! thou art too dear for my possessing,
And like enough thou know'st thy estimate:
The charter of thy worth gives thee releasing;
My bonds in thee are all determinate.
For how do I hold thee but by thy granting?
And for that riches where is my deserving?
The cause of this fair gift in me is wanting,
And so my patent back again is swerving.
Thyself thou gavest, thy own worth then not knowing,
Or me, to whom thou gavest it, else mistaking;
So thy great gift, upon misprision growing,
Comes home again, on better judgment making.
    Thus have I had thee, as a dream doth flatter,
    In sleep a king, but waking no such matter.

LXXXVIII

When thou shalt be disposed to set me light,
And place my merit in the eye of scorn,
Upon thy side against myself I'll fight,
And prove thee virtuous, though thou art forsworn.
With mine own weakness being best acquainted,
Upon thy part I can set down a story
Of faults conceal'd, wherein I am attainted,
That thou in losing me shalt win much glory:
And I by this will be a gainer too;
For bending all my loving thoughts on thee,
The injuries that to myself I do,
Doing thee vantage, double-vantage me.
    Such is my love, to thee I so belong,
    That for thy right myself will bear all wrong.

87 *That's It! Finito! I Can't Hold On To You.*

¡ Adios ! Thou art too costly for my owning,
and probably thou know'st how much thou'rt worth;
thy worth's an out-of-jail with royal crowning;
my bonds in you run out, no bodying forth.
For how do I hold you but by your granting?
And for that windfall, what's my justifying?
No grounds for this fair gift! for I am wanting,
and so my warrant fails, and flops back, dying.
You hung with Will, your gift's high worth not knowing,
donor! or possibly my worth mistaking;
so your vast gift, upon misprision growing,
turns back to you, on right appraisal-making.
    Having you was a thrill, a king's nocturnal
    fantasia; but no such thing, diurnal.

88 *I'll support you in your calumny: it's win-win.*

That day rolls on, that you'll inflict a slight,
arraign my quiddity in courts of scorn.
For you I'll altruistically fight,
proving you virtuous, though thou art forsworn.
Of my own failings I'm most cognizant,
and to your gain I can submit a story
of faults of which mankind is ignorant:
thus by my loss you stand to win much glory.
And by this I shall gain much profit too,
so, turning all my loving thoughts your way,
this autoblaptic injury I'll do.
You'll gain, I'll gain twofold: 'twill triply pay.
    I'm yours: for you, my loving is so strong
    that for your right, I'll ship a load of wrong.

Autoblaptic: I'm my injury's origin.

LXXXIX

Say that thou didst forsake me for some fault,
And I will comment upon that offence;
Speak of my lameness, and I straight will halt,
Against thy reasons making no defence.
Thou canst not, love, disgrace me half so ill,
To set a form upon desired change,
As I'll myself disgrace: knowing thy will,
I will acquaintance strangle and look strange,
Be absent from thy walks, and in my tongue
Thy sweet beloved name no more shall dwell,
Lest I, too much profane, should do it wrong
And haply of our old acquaintance tell.
 For thee against myself I'll vow debate,
 For I must ne'er love him whom thou dost hate.

XC

Then hate me when thou wilt; if ever, now;
Now, while the world is bent my deeds to cross,
Join with the spite of fortune, make me bow,
And do not drop in for an after-loss:
Ah, do not, when my heart hath 'scoped this sorrow,
Come in the rearward of a conquer'd woe;
 Give not a windy night a rainy morrow,
To linger out a purposed overthrow.
If thou wilt leave me, do not leave me last,
When other petty griefs have done their spite,
But in the onset come; so shall I taste
At first the very worst of fortune's might,
 And other strains of woe, which now seem woe,
 Compared with loss of thee will not seem so.

89 *Anything bad you say about yours-truly,*
I'll confirm.

Say you forsook yours-truly for my fault,
and I'll indict my own iniquity;
Say I can't walk, and straightaway I'll halt,
not contradict at all your obloquy.
You cannot damn yours-truly half so ill,
calling for thorough-going transformation,
as autocritic I... I know your will:
strangling old bonds, changing my figuration,
I shall avoid your walks, and on my lip
your darling monica shall gain no grip:
I might impugn it, for a guy can slip
up: I might talk of our companionship.
    For you I vow my words will work my loss,
    not loving him whom you think odious.

90 *If you want to go, go quickly.*

So, I am odious: act upon it now!
Now, whilst all things concur my plans to cross,
join vicious Lady Luck, and I'll kowtow.
Don't wait around to inflict a knock-on loss;
don't, if my spirit has outrun this sorrow,
attack, in flank or back, a pain outgrown;
don't add to windy night a rainy morrow,
slowing and drawing out my groan and moan.
If you pull out for good, don't pull out last,
small sundry vicious pains impinging first:
no, attack first: and I shall savour fast
(and first) what Lady Luck can do, at worst.
    And pains that now may show what pains can do
    won't stand comparison with losing you.

XCI

Some glory in their birth, some in their skill,
Some in their wealth, some in their bodies' force,
Some in their garments, though new-fangled ill,
Some in their hawks and hounds, some in their horse;
And every humour hath his adjunct pleasure,
Wherein it finds a joy above the rest:
But these particulars are not my measure;
All these I better in one general best.
Thy love is better than high birth to me,
Richer than wealth, prouder than garments' cost,
Of more delight than hawks or horses be;
And having thee, of all men's pride I boast:
    Wretched in this alone, that thou mayst take
    All this away and me most wretched make.

XCII

But do thy worst to steal thyself away,
For term of life thou art assured mine,
And life no longer than thy love will stay,
For it depends upon that love of thine.
Then need I not to fear the worst of wrongs,
When in the least of them my life hath end.
I see a better state to me belongs
Than that which on thy humour doth depend;
Thou canst not vex me with inconstant mind,
Since that my life on thy revolt doth lie.
O, what a happy title do I find,
Happy to have thy love, happy to die!
    But what's so blessed-fair that fears no blot?
    Thou mayst be false, and yet I know it not.

91 *I glory in your loving, that's what I'm proud of.*

Glory in birth, lad, glory too in skill,
glory in gilts and cash, in limbs of oak,
glory in clothing, fancy fashion's frill,
glory in prancing stallion, hound and hawk;
and any whimsy has its joy adjoint,
a joy that hits a vying rival hard.
But such particulars I do not want:
outdoing all, I play my winning card.
Your loving in my book outranks high birth,
outgilding gilts, outshouting clothing's cost,
outhounding hounds, outrunning stallions' worth;
and having you, how proudly do I boast!
    Only in this most sorry, that you may
    withdraw it all, on my most sorry day.

92 *Loving, Losing, and Mortality*

But do your worst, go skulking on your way,
I hold you firm, as long as I am living;
my living shall your loving not outstay:
it cannot last without your loving's thriving.
I'm not afraid of any monstrous wrong,
for your most tiny wrong my star can dim.
I know my lucky star should flourish strong:
it shouldn't only hang upon your whim.
You can't harass me with inconstant mind:
I just put up with your apostasy.
O what a happy station do I find:
your loving, passing out, mortality!
    But what good luck is wary of no blot?
    You may turn traitor, and I know it not.

XCIII

So shall I live, supposing thou art true,
Like a deceived husband; so love's face
May still seem love to me, though alter'd new;
Thy looks with me, thy heart in other place:
For there can live no hatred in thine eye,
Therefore in that I cannot know thy change.
In many's looks the false heart's history
Is writ in moods and frowns and wrinkles strange,
But heaven in thy creation did decree
That in thy face sweet love should ever dwell;
Whate'er thy thoughts or thy heart's workings be,
Thy looks should nothing thence but sweetness tell.
　　How like Eve's apple doth thy beauty grow,
　　if thy sweet virtue answer not thy show!

XCIV

They that have power to hurt and will do none,
That do not do the thing they most do show,
Who, moving others, are themselves as stone,
Unmoved, cold, and to temptation slow,
They rightly do inherit heaven's graces
And husband nature's riches from expense;
They are the lords and owners of their faces,
Others but stewards of their excellence.
The summer's flower is to the summer sweet,
Though to itself it only live and die,
But if that flower with base infection meet,
The basest weed outbraves his dignity:
　　For sweetest things turn sourest by their deeds;
　　Lilies that fester smell far worse than weeds.

93 Two-Timing? Your Looks Don't Show It

Think of a cuckold! I shall carry on,
imagining you loyal. So I'll still
call you my darling, though you morph anon:
your looks, but not your longings, stay with Will.
I cannot study your inconstancy,
for signs of loathing do not cross your brow.
On many brows, a turncoat's history
is writ in moods and frowns and wrinkly show.
But God Almighty, making you, has wrought
yours always loving, not at all unkind:
a charming sight, ignoring any thought
and any inclinations of your mind.
    You! Far from virtuous! Vivacious, youthful:
    I think of Madam Adam's sinful mouthful!

94 A Complaint about Withholding

Folk that can wound at will, and will not wound,
not doing what is obviously on show,
though moving us, as cold as stony ground,
cold and unmoving, loth to sink so low:
such folk incur a bounty from on high
and guard a natural boon from dissipation,
owning by right a physiognomy,
lords, not just bailiffs, of its coruscation.
A bloom in May gifts May its rich aroma,
focusing just on living and mortality;
but if that bloom contracts a foul sarcoma,
any low wort outrivals it for quality.
    Things sugary turn sour by vicious works:
    a rotting lily stinks out fifty worts.

XCV

How sweet and lovely dost thou make the shame
Which, like a canker in the fragrant rose,
Doth spot the beauty of thy budding name!
O, in what sweets dost thou thy sins enclose!
That tongue that tells the story of thy days,
Making lascivious comments on thy sport,
Cannot dispraise but in a kind of praise;
Naming thy name blesses an ill report.
O, what a mansion have those vices got
Which for their habitation chose out thee,
Where beauty's veil doth cover every blot,
And all things turn to fair that eyes can see!
   Take heed, dear heart, of this large privilege;
   The hardest knife ill-used doth lose his edge.

XCVI

Some say thy fault is youth, some wantonness;
Some say thy grace is youth and gentle sport;
Both grace and faults are loved of more and less;
Thou makest faults graces that to thee resort.
As on the finger of a throned queen
The basest jewel will be well esteem'd,
So are those errors that in thee are seen
To truths translated and for true things deem'd.
How many lambs might the stern wolf betray,
If like a lamb he could his looks translate!
How many gazers mightst thou lead away,
If thou wouldst use the strength of all thy state!
   But do not so; I love thee in such sort
   As, thou being mine, mine is thy good report.

95 *Your good looks disarm criticism. Watch out, though!*

What charm you bring to your dishonour, that,
as would a maggot in a fragrant bloom,
corrupts your halo's rosy bud! And what
charms mask your sins, as in a tight-shut room!
Such biographic lips as blurt your story,
talking lasciviously of your pranks,
can't knock you: knocking turns out laudatory:
naming you turns bad odour sacrosanct.
O! what a mansion has that frailty got
which for its habitation lit on you,
for, pulchritudinously, any blot
is hid from sight: all's fair, and wants to woo.
    Watch out, my darling, with your whopping gift:
    sharp shivs, ill-swung, go blunt. D'you catch my drift?

96 *Opinions About Your Faults and Charms*

Your fault is variously youth or lust,
your charm is variously youth and chuckling,
with both, you charm plain folk and fancy crust;
you turn faults into charms, a swansdown duckling.
As, on a royal pinky proudly stuck,
a zircon would obtain high valuation,
so your shortcomings and distortions look
truthful, and win a ringing vindication.
How many lambs might th' unkind wolf undo,
if wolf could turn from wolf into a lamb!
How many gawping souls might follow you,
if you'd apply your maximum grand slam!
    Don't do it, though: you know my caring humour:
    I hold you tight, and hold off ugly rumour.

XCVII

How like a winter hath my absence been
 From thee, the pleasure of the fleeting year!
What freezings have I felt, what dark days seen!
What old December's bareness every where!
And yet this time removed was summer's time,
The teeming autumn, big with rich increase,
Bearing the wanton burden of the prime,
Like widow'd wombs after their lords' decease:
Yet this abundant issue seem'd to me
But hope of orphans and unfather'd fruit;
For summer and his pleasures wait on thee,
And, thou away, the very birds are mute;
    Or, if they sing, 'tis with so dull a cheer
    That leaves look pale, dreading the winter's near.

XCVIII

From you have I been absent in the spring,
When proud-pied April dress'd in all his trim
Hath put a spirit of youth in every thing,
That heavy Saturn laugh'd and leap'd with him.
Yet nor the lays of birds nor the sweet smell
Of different flowers in odour and in hue
Could make me any summer's story tell,
Or from their proud lap pluck them where they grew;
Nor did I wonder at the lily's white,
Nor praise the deep vermilion in the rose;
They were but sweet, but figures of delight,
Drawn after you, you pattern of all those.
    Yet seem'd it winter still, and, you away,
    As with your shadow I with these did play.

97 It's Cold And I'm Missing You

Think of a wintry chill! I'm missing you,
my joy as months and days shot swiftly on;
such icy cold: dark days, and dismal too,
bad old Jack Frost, and boughs with nothing on.
My actual loss was August and July,
and gravid autumn, big with goodly hoard,
wanton accrual of tumidity,
womb of a widow with no living lord.
Abundant output! But it wouldn't do,
I thought of fruits mis-born, an orphan crop:
all warm days' joys must follow on from you;
with you away, why, birdsong's bound to stop,
    or flop and flag, not glorious nor bold,
      and oaks shrink pallid from approaching cold.

98 Spring was Just a Pallid Imitation

From you I was far distant. It was spring,
and April proud in panchromatic trim
had put a spurt of youth on anything;
Saturn was laughing, jumping round with him.
But birdsong couldn't, nor could fragrant odour
of blooms of various colours, turn your chap
into a dog-days, warm July narrator;
nor would I pluck a bud from blooms' proud lap,
nor did I gasp at sight of snowy lily,
nor drool at * 'Crimson Glory', 'Cramoisi',
both colours drawn from you originally,
now disappointing, lacking brilliancy.
    I thought: still January! Had to play
      with buds, as with your shadow, far away.

Hybrids found in many a plant catalog.

XCIX

The forward violet thus did I chide:
Sweet thief, whence didst thou steal thy sweet that smells,
If not from my love's breath? The purple pride
Which on thy soft cheek for complexion dwells
In my love's veins thou hast too grossly dyed.
The lily I condemned for thy hand,
And buds of marjoram had stol'n thy hair:
The roses fearfully on thorns did stand,
 One blushing shame, another white despair;
A third, nor red nor white, had stol'n of both
And to his robbery had annex'd thy breath;
But, for his theft, in pride of all his growth
A vengeful canker eat him up to death.
  More flowers I noted, yet I none could see
  But sweet or colour it had stol'n from thee.

C

Where art thou, Muse, that thou forget'st so long
To speak of that which gives thee all thy might?
Spend'st thou thy fury on some worthless song,
Darkening thy power to lend base subjects light?
Return, forgetful Muse, and straight redeem
In gentle numbers time so idly spent;
Sing to the ear that doth thy lays esteem
And gives thy pen both skill and argument.
Rise, resty Muse, my love's sweet face survey,
If Time have any wrinkle graven there;
If any, be a satire to decay,
And make Time's spoils despised every where.
  Give my love fame faster than Time wastes life;
  So thou prevent'st his scythe and crooked knife.

99 Botany's Burglars

A Parma bloom was brash. Did I upbraid!
'You fragrant burglar! Is that yours, (I said)
that odour? It's my darling's! And that tint,
porphyry-proud, which on your mug is laid?
You grossly took that colour from my bint.'
I chid a lily, too, about your hand,
and buds of marjoram that filch your hair;
blushing and blanching blooms on thorns did stand,
Lancastrian and Yorkist, shifty pair.
A Tudor third had got a bit of both,
adding your lungs' soft vapour to his gains:
but tit for tat, for all his vaunting growth,
an angry blight unstrung him, for his pains!
    I saw a lot of blooms, all guilty too:
    burglars, who all got tint or tang from you.

Bint (Arabic): girl; also connoting kinship with papa.
Probably, though, Will has his young man in mind.

100 A Call for Inspiration to Furnish Aid, as of Old.

My lyrical Parnassian! Why so long
away from what affords you all your might?
Wasting your passion on a rubbish song,
dimming your bulb and making trivia bright?
Turn, turn, oblivious Lady, clawing back
in my mild stanzas all your lazy days;
sing to this auditor who has both knack
and topic for you, and applauds your lays.
Up, idling Lady, scan my darling's brow:
has Old Man Ticktock dug a sulculus?
if so, you'll wax satirical, and lo!
scorn of his spoiling grows ubiquitous.
    Puff my chuck's glory quick as Clock runs slow:
    thwart his sharp cuts, obstruct his wounding blow.

Sulculus: Latin word for a small furrow.

CI

O truant Muse, what shall be thy amends
For thy neglect of truth in beauty dyed?
Both truth and beauty on my love depends;
So dost thou too, and therein dignified.
Make answer, Muse: wilt thou not haply say
'Truth needs no colour, with his colour fix'd;
Beauty no pencil, beauty's truth to lay;
But best is best, if never intermix'd?'
Because he needs no praise, wilt thou be dumb?
Excuse not silence so; for't lies in thee
To make him much outlive a gilded tomb,
And to be praised of ages yet to be.
   Then do thy office, Muse; I teach thee how
   To make him seem long hence as he shows now.

CII

My love is strengthen'd, though more weak in seeming;
I love not less, though less the show appear:
That love is merchandized whose rich esteeming
The owner's tongue doth publish every where.
Our love was new and then but in the spring
When I was wont to greet it with my lays,
As Philomel in summer's front doth sing
And stops her pipe in growth of riper days:
Not that the summer is less pleasant now
Than when her mournful hymns did hush the night,
But that wild music burthens every bough
And sweets grown common lose their dear delight.
   Therefore like her I sometime hold my tongue,
   Because I would not dull you with my song.

101 Do your job, inspiring child of Apollo!

You sold Truth short, Parnassian, as you sang!
For Truth was dipt in Kallos' gaudy vat.
Both Truth and Kallos on my loving hang,
and so do you: your Kudos hails from that.
Lady, in mitigation you may say:
'Truth wants no colour, with his colour fixt,
Kallos no stylus for his truth-display.
Good upshot, if this pair is not commixt.'
My guy's past praising: do you just go dumb?
Don't try to gloss your taciturnity;
allow him to outlast a cold gold tomb,
gain plaudits through unfolding history.
    So, Lady, do your job: I'll show you how:
    his looks in far-off days shall charm as now.

Kallos: good looks. Kudos: high standing.
Words known to Plato.

102 A famous songbird, and I,
may not always sing.

My loving grows, you might think it is fading,
my loving wasn't shrunk, don't think it was.
Loving blown loud is only good for trading,
broadcast by raucous boss, ubiquitous.
Our loving got a start, was still in spring
as I was wont to laud it with my lays;
so Itys' bird in month of May doth sing,
and stops its larynx in maturing days.
I do think August's just as joyful now,
without that sad bird's lullaby at night;
but its wild music loads too many a bough;
and joys too common, cloying, turn to blight.
    Now and again, I too may not prolong
    my music, not to dull you with my song.

Itys' bird: rossignol, Nachtigall (story told by Ovid).

CIII

Alack, what poverty my Muse brings forth,
That having such a scope to show her pride,
The argument all bare is of more worth
Than when it hath my added praise beside!
O, blame me not, if I no more can write!
Look in your glass, and there appears a face
That over-goes my blunt invention quite,
Dulling my lines and doing me disgrace.
Were it not sinful then, striving to mend,
To mar the subject that before was well?
For to no other pass my verses tend
Than of your graces and your gifts to tell;
    And more, much more, than in my verse can sit
    Your own glass shows you when you look in it.

CIV

To me, fair friend, you never can be old,
For as you were when first your eye I eyed,
Such seems your beauty still. Three winters cold
Have from the forests shook three summers' pride,
Three beauteous springs to yellow autumn turn'd
In process of the seasons have I seen,
Three April perfumes in three hot Junes burn'd,
Since first I saw you fresh, which yet are green.
Ah! yet doth beauty, like a dial-hand,
Steal from his figure and no pace perceived;
So your sweet hue, which methinks still doth stand,
Hath motion and mine eye may be deceived:
    For fear of which, hear this, thou age unbred;
    Ere you were born was beauty's summer dead.

103 *All this is Too Much for my Poor Ability.*

Alack! What dross my Guiding Star brings forth,
with such an opportunity to win!
My topic in its basic form is worth
as much as with my plaudits all thrown in.
It's not my fault at all if I'm struck dumb!
Look in your mirror, and you'll find a mazzard
that far outruns my blunt arbitrium,
dulls all my stanzas, puts my gloss at hazard.
So I'd do wrong if, striving to adjust,
I'd spoil a topic that was A-OK.
It is my stanzas' solitary thrust
to hymn your gifts, your bull points, I may say.
    You so outclass what in my book can sit!
    Your own glass shows you, if you look in it.

Mazzard: physiognomy.
Arbitrium: wisdom, discrimination.

104 *You look just as you always did. But...*

Chuck, in my book you can't and won't grow old:
you look just as you did that day I first
saw you: so pulchritudinous. A cold
January shook from wildwoods August's burst
of glory; autumn gold stood in for spring;
April's aromas burnt in hot July,
again, again I saw that annual swing!
It was that long ago. You still look spry!
But, ah! chic charm's a crawling dial-hand,
slips past its digit, much too slow to spot;
so your bright colours, which in my sight stand
static, go moving: spot which, I may not.
    So I'm afraid. Hark, all you days unborn!
    Youth didn't wait: its warmth burnt out, forlorn.

CV

Let not my love be call'd idolatry,
Nor my beloved as an idol show,
Since all alike my songs and praises be
To one, of one, still such, and ever so.
Kind is my love to-day, to-morrow kind,
Still constant in a wondrous excellence;
Therefore my verse to constancy confined,
One thing expressing, leaves out difference.
'Fair, kind and true' is all my argument,
'Fair, kind, and true' varying to other words;
And in this change is my invention spent,
Three themes in one, which wondrous scope affords.
    'Fair, kind, and true' have often lived alone,
    Which three till now never kept seat in one.

CVI

When in the chronicle of wasted time
I see descriptions of the fairest wights,
And beauty making beautiful old rhyme
In praise of ladies dead and lovely knights,
Then, in the blazon of sweet beauty's best
Of hand, of foot, of lip, of eye, of brow,
I see their antique pen would have express'd
Even such a beauty as you master now.
So all their praises are but prophecies
Of this our time, all you prefiguring;
And, for they look'd but with divining eyes,
They had not skill enough your worth to sing:
    For we, which now behold these present days,
    Had eyes to wonder, but lack tongues to praise.

105 *Adoring a Unitary Trio*

Don't anybody say 'idolatry';
don't say my darling is an idol. No,
for all my songs laud indivisibly
A unity, still such and always so.
My chuck is kind today, tomorrow kind,
still constant, with a wondrous quiddity;
and so I sing with constancy in mind,
I focus to omit all oddity.
'Groovy, kind, constant' is my story's plot,
'Groovy, kind, constant' said in various ways:
and varying this trilogy is what
I put my skills to, for it plays, and pays.
    'Groovy, kind, constant': any on its own
    Is normal: but a trio? That's unknown!

106 *History's All About You*

If in old annals of far distant days
I find accounts of dishy-looking churls,
good looks on which old wordsmiths built good lays,
bigging up hunky knights and smashing girls,
this I know: blazoning top quality
of hand, of foot, of lip, of orb, of brow,
historic quills had full capacity
to limn such classic form as yours is now.
All that old stuff is just anticipation
of us today: it's all to do with you:
not living, but a rough approximation,
a portrait-job that nobody could do.
    Among us now you look miraculous:
    our poor acclaim's in no way congruous.

CVII

Not mine own fears, nor the prophetic soul
Of the wide world dreaming on things to come,
Can yet the lease of my true love control,
Supposed as forfeit to a confined doom.
The mortal moon hath her eclipse endured
And the sad augurs mock their own presage;
Incertainties now crown themselves assured
And peace proclaims olives of endless age.
Now with the drops of this most balmy time
My love looks fresh, and death to me subscribes,
Since, spite of him, I'll live in this poor rhyme,
While he insults o'er dull and speechless tribes:
    And thou in this shalt find thy monument,
    When tyrants' crests and tombs of brass are spent.

CVIII

What's in the brain that ink may character
Which hath not figured to thee my true spirit?
What's new to speak, what new to register,
That may express my love or thy dear merit?
Nothing, sweet boy; but yet, like prayers divine,
I must, each day say o'er the very same,
Counting no old thing old, thou mine, I thine,
Even as when first I hallow'd thy fair name.
So that eternal love in love's fresh case
Weighs not the dust and injury of age,
Nor gives to necessary wrinkles place,
But makes antiquity for aye his page,
    Finding the first conceit of love there bred
    Where time and outward form would show it dead.

107 *Your Immortality in my Words*

Not my misgivings, nor this vast world's soul,
Clairvoyant, musing on futurity,
can bring my loving-span within control,
in pawn to prison of mortality.
Now mortal moon has known its black occlusion,
sad augurs mock old words of doom miscast,
doubts put on crowns abjuring all confusion,
orchards flaunt fruits pacific. Conflict's past.
My darling's blooming in this balmy day!
What of old Dis? I'm not afraid of him:
I'll last by my poor rhyming, anyway,
whilst Dis shall bully folk too dumb, too dim.
    Through this, your tumulus shall long surpass
    Vain tyrants' coats-of-arms and tombs of brass.

Dis, or Pluto: grim god of Tartarus.

108 *What can I add? I'll say my words again...*

What's in my brain that ink may body forth
which hasn't shown you all my cast of thought?
What can I add, what affidavit's worth
a try, loving you, darling, as I ought?
Nothing at all; but still, this litany,
as would a monk or parson, I must say
daily, and count no old thing old, for I
am yours, and own you, from our first saint's-day.
Thus my unfading worship, always bright,
won't sag with hoary dust and injury,
won't grant obtruding furrows any right;
anchors its writing in antiquity,
    that brought to birth our first purport of loving,
    which clocks and outward form would mourn unmoving.

CIX

O, never say that I was false of heart,
Though absence seem'd my flame to qualify.
As easy might I from myself depart
As from my soul, which in thy breast doth lie:
That is my home of love: if I have ranged,
Like him that travels I return again,
Just to the time, not with the time exchanged,
So that myself bring water for my stain.
Never believe, though in my nature reign'd
All frailties that besiege all kinds of blood,
That it could so preposterously be stain'd,
To leave for nothing all thy sum of good;
 For nothing this wide universe I call,
 Save thou, my rose; in it thou art my all.

CX

Alas, 'tis true I have gone here and there
And made myself a motley to the view,
 Gored mine own thoughts, sold cheap what is most dear,
Made old offences of affections new;
Most true it is that I have look'd on truth
Askance and strangely: but, by all above,
These blenches gave my heart another youth,
And worse essays proved thee my best of love.
Now all is done, have what shall have no end:
Mine appetite I never more will grind
On newer proof, to try an older friend,
A god in love, to whom I am confined.
 Then give me welcome, next my heaven the best,
 Even to thy pure and most most loving breast.

109 *Don't say I was disloyal during our days apart...*

O! do not say that I disloyal was!
Far off from you, could my torch gallivant?
I could as simply from Yours Truly pass
as from my soul, your bosom's occupant.
That is my loving's focus: did I stray?
If so, your tourist has got back again,
and punctually too, right hour, right day,
so I can quickly wash away my stain.
But don't think any nasty frailty got
control - it can assail all kinds of blood -
that I could so absurdly ship a blot,
and quit for nothing all your sum of good.
   In this vast cosmos, nothing! that's my call:
   just rosy thou: in it thou art my all.

110 *Now I Know to Abstain*

I must admit I shook it all about,
I was a fool, and most conspicuous,
sold gold-dust for a song, was foul of thought,
an innovator drably scandalous.
What is most truthful is that I saw truth
with an odd squint: but oh, by jiminy!
Such pallors brought my blood-pump vital youth,
bad probings proving your good quality.
So much for that. This gift is yours for good:
I shall not grind again my inclination
on unknown try-outs that would try your mood,
you god of loving, you my grand fixation.
   So! Now to hug your bosom, most of all,
   most staunch and loving on this old round ball.

CXI

O, for my sake do you with Fortune chide,
The guilty goddess of my harmful deeds,
That did not better for my life provide
Than public means which public manners breeds.
Thence comes it that my name receives a brand,
And almost thence my nature is subdued
To what it works in, like the dyer's hand:
Pity me then and wish I were renew'd;
Whilst, like a willing patient, I will drink
Potions of eisel 'gainst my strong infection;
No bitterness that I will bitter think,
Nor double penance, to correct correction.
   Pity me then, dear friend, and I assure ye
   Even that your pity is enough to cure me.

CXII

Your love and pity doth the impression fill
Which vulgar scandal stamp'd upon my brow;
For what care I who calls me well or ill,
So you o'er-green my bad, my good allow?
You are my all the world, and I must strive
To know my shames and praises from your tongue:
None else to me, nor I to none alive,
That my steel'd sense or changes right or wrong.
In so profound abysm I throw all care
Of others' voices, that my adder's sense
To critic and to flatterer stopped are.
Mark how with my neglect I do dispense:
   You are so strongly in my purpose bred
   That all the world besides methinks are dead.

111 *I must work, must dirty my hands.*
Pity my failings!

Go, carp on my account at Lady Luck,
that diva, guilty of my harmful ways,
by whom with working for my crust I'm stuck:
a working man, my conduct so displays.
That's why my monica has got a brand,
and why my spirit's almost brought right down
to what it works in, as a tintsman's hand.
It's pitiful: so, wish my plight outgrown,
whilst for my doctor willingly I'll drink
castor oil potions 'gainst contamination,
call no draught nasty, no punitions think
too much, for castigating castigation.
  So, pity your good chum, with my assuring.
  your pity on its own can work my curing.

Tintsman: his job is to dip cloth in vats of various colours.

112 *No Gossip – Just You, to Discuss My Faults*

Your loving pity had a scar to fill,
which vulgar scandal dug into my brow.
I don't mind gossip on my good or ill:
my bad you'll airbrush, and my good, allow.
My total world is you: and I must try
to know my good and bad by your straight shooting:
to nobody, and just from you, can my
strict guard admit of right or wrong's imputing.
Down chasms most profound I throw all thought
of third opinions, aurally blot out
critic and sycophant: no hint is caught.
You'll mark, how nonchalant my walkabout!
  You grow so strongly in my plans, that all
  mankind, but you, incurs a dying fall.

CXIII

Since I left you, mine eye is in my mind;
And that which governs me to go about
Doth part his function and is partly blind,
Seems seeing, but effectually is out;
For it no form delivers to the heart
Of bird, of flower, or shape, which it doth latch:
Of his quick objects hath the mind no part,
Nor his own vision holds what it doth catch:
For if it see the rudest or gentlest sight,
The most sweet favour or deformed'st creature,
The mountain or the sea, the day or night,
The crow or dove, it shapes them to your feature:
    Incapable of more, replete with you,
      My most true mind thus makes mine eye untrue.

CXIV

Or whether doth my mind, being crown'd with you,
Drink up the monarch's plague, this flattery?
Or whether shall I say, mine eye saith true,
And that your love taught it this alchemy,
To make of monsters and things indigest
Such cherubins as your sweet self resemble,
Creating every bad a perfect best,
As fast as objects to his beams assemble?
O, 'tis the first; 'tis flattery in my seeing,
And my great mind most kingly drinks it up:
Mine eye well knows what with his gust is 'greeing,
And to his palate doth prepare the cup:
    If it be poison'd, 'tis the lesser sin
      That mine eye loves it and doth first begin.

113 Sight and mind: if I look at anything, it turns into you.

Away from you, my sight is in my mind:
what should control my strings to go about
parts from its function and is partly blind,
looks as if looking, but in fact is out:
for it transmits no form into my brain
of bird, of bloom, or solid thing, but naught:
all moving things approach my mind in vain;
it can't hold in its vision what it's caught.
For if it spots any most utmost sight,
most rough or smooth, most gibbous or most gracious,
mountain or briny main, bright day, dark night,
crow, swan, it turns all into your bodacious
     phiz. That's my maximum! Of you, I'm full,
     mind's duty making sight undutiful.

114 My Sight or my Mind: which is at Fault in this?

Has my mind worn your crown monarchical
to drink this sycophancy, blight of kings?
Or shall I say my sight is dutiful,
taught by my loving to do wondrous things,
transforming warthogs and amorphous dough
into sky-spirits glorious, of your kind,
making from bad a most magnifico,
homing on things as fast as it can find?
O! it is sycophancy in my sight,
and my high mind most kingly drinks it up:
my sight is skilful, knows what flavour's right
for my mind's buds, and thus distils his cup:
     and if it's poison, that's not such a sin:
     my sight is first, and lovingly tucks in!

CXV

Those lines that I before have writ do lie,
Even those that said I could not love you dearer:
Yet then my judgment knew no reason why
My most full flame should afterwards burn clearer.
But reckoning time, whose million'd accidents
Creep in 'twixt vows and change decrees of kings,
Tan sacred beauty, blunt the sharp'st intents,
Divert strong minds to the course of altering things;
Alas, why, fearing of time's tyranny,
Might I not then say 'Now I love you best,'
When I was certain o'er incertainty,
Crowning the present, doubting of the rest?
   Love is a babe; then might I not say so,
   To give full growth to that which still doth grow?

CXVI

Let me not to the marriage of true minds
Admit impediments. Love is not love
Which alters when it alteration finds,
Or bends with the remover to remove:
O no! it is an ever-fixed mark
That looks on tempests and is never shaken;
It is the star to every wandering bark,
Whose worth's unknown, although his height be taken.
Love's not Time's fool, though rosy lips and cheeks
Within his bending sickle's compass come:
Love alters not with his brief hours and weeks,
But bears it out even to the edge of doom.
   If this be error and upon me proved,
   I never writ, nor no man ever loved.

115 *I said my Loving was at a Maximum.*
I was Wrong!

My prior writing partly misinform:
I said I couldn't up my notch of loving.
I hadn't any grounds to think my warm
bright torch's brilliancy was still improving.
But Clock with million random small disposals
crawls in 'twixt vows, distorts commands of kings,
stains holy charm of form, blunts sharp proposals,
draws off strong minds to track inconstant things.
Alas! Afraid of Tick-Tock's tyranny,
I said - and why not? – 'Now I'm most adoring,'
for I was firm on Luck's infirmity,
crowning that hour, futurity abjuring.
    Amor's a baby: shouldn't I say so,
      to grant full growth to that which still doth grow?

116 *Admit No Obstruction*

Don't block a union of two loving minds.
Fond adoration's not fond adoration
which flips as soon as it mutation finds,
or flops at any discontinuation.
Oh no! It is a constant mark, that stays,
looking at storms, and still as statuary:
a guiding star to any ship that strays.
(How high? That's known. What is it, though? Don't worry!)
It's no clock's fool, though clocks watch rosy lips
wilt, as a day cuts corn: that day's short room
won't vary it, nor will a month that slips
rapidly past. It lasts till crack of doom.
    If I am wrong on this, and proofs obtain,
      no wordsmith I, and Cupid shoots in vain.

CXVII

Accuse me thus: that I have scanted all
Wherein I should your great deserts repay,
Forgot upon your dearest love to call,
Whereto all bonds do tie me day by day;
That I have frequent been with unknown minds
And given to time your own dear-purchased right
That I have hoisted sail to all the winds
Which should transport me farthest from your sight.
Book both my wilfulness and errors down
And on just proof surmise accumulate;
Bring me within the level of your frown,
But shoot not at me in your waken'd hate;
    Since my appeal says I did strive to prove
    The constancy and virtue of your love.

CXVIII

Like as, to make our appetites more keen,
With eager compounds we our palate urge,
As, to prevent our maladies unseen,
We sicken to shun sickness when we purge,
Even so, being full of your ne'er-cloying sweetness,
To bitter sauces did I frame my feeding
And, sick of welfare, found a kind of meetness
To be diseased ere that there was true needing.
Thus policy in love, to anticipate
The ills that were not, grew to faults assured
And brought to medicine a healthful state
Which, rank of goodness, would by ill be cured:
    But thence I learn, and find the lesson true,
    Drugs poison him that so fell sick of you.

117 OK, Bring a Criminal Action! – but I'll say...

Indict my wrongs: say I paid short for all
your comity, which I should justly pay;
on your warm loving I forgot to call,
to which I'm tightly bound, both night and day;
I was companion too to unknown minds,
giving away your costly-bought own right,
and hoisting sail to all and any winds
that might transport my craft far from your sight.
Book all my wilful ways and failings down,
stack up on just proof lots of supposition;
bring Will within your gunsights as you frown,
don't shoot, though, in your furibund condition;
    I'll claim what I was striving for was proving
    your constancy, your honour in your loving.

118 I took a bit of Tasty Stuff, but...

Just as, to polish up his lust for food,
a man may goad his buds with spicy stuff;
or, to thwart malady and stay in good,
condition, go down sick by purging tough:
so I, full up with your uncloying sugar,
took to consumption of acidulous
flavours, and sick of fussing, found a vigour
in ailing, though it far from crucial was.
That's crafty loving! That's anticipating
imaginary ills. So things got squalid: I
undid my good condition, rank with sating
sugars, and I was put to rights by malady.
    But do I draw a moral? Oh, I do:
    drugs poison him that got so sick of you.

CXIX

What potions have I drunk of Siren tears,
Distill'd from limbecks foul as hell within,
Applying fears to hopes and hopes to fears,
Still losing when I saw myself to win!
What wretched errors hath my heart committed,
Whilst it hath thought itself so blessed never!
How have mine eyes out of their spheres been fitted
 In the distraction of this madding fever!
O benefit of ill! now I find true
That better is by evil still made better;
And ruin'd love, when it is built anew,
Grows fairer than at first, more strong, far greater.
  So I return rebuked to my content
  And gain by ill thrice more than I have spent.

CXX

That you were once unkind befriends me now,
And for that sorrow which I then did feel
Needs must I under my transgression bow,
Unless my nerves were brass or hammer'd steel.
For if you were by my unkindness shaken
As I by yours, you've pass'd a hell of time,
And I, a tyrant, have no leisure taken
To weigh how once I suffered in your crime.
O, that our night of woe might have remember'd
My deepest sense, how hard true sorrow hits,
And soon to you, as you to me, then tender'd
The humble salve which wounded bosoms fits!
  But that your trespass now becomes a fee;
  Mine ransoms yours, and yours must ransom me.

119 It's Nasty, but it Works!

So many potions drunk, which fays had laid
sobbing in Satan's cups, foul atropin!
Afraid but trusting, trusting but afraid,
I was still losing, though I thought to win.
What dismal faults, from amorous longing sprung!
To think I thought I was in world-class luck!
Both of my orbs out of both orbits wrung:
wild horror of this quinsy, run amuck!
Profit from not-so-fit! and so I found
that bad can add to good, in fact can grow it:
and loving brought to nought can upward bound,
built back again, fair, strong, and still outdo it.
   So I go back, told off but far from sorry,
   triply quids-in, from gains non-salutary.

Amuck: a Malay word: crazy, frantic.
In strict orthography, it is 'amok'.

120 It has hurt us both.

Your prior unkind act's my buddy now,
and for my sorrow that was congruous
I'm cringing for my guilt, I humbly bow,
not having cast-iron ganglia, nor brass.
If you as much at my misconduct shook
as I at yours, your pain was harrowing;
and I, tyrannical, no lunch-hours took,
but thought about my sorrow at your fling.
I wish in that sad night my inmost mind
had known again how hard stark sorrows hit:
and you and I could mutually mind
our bosoms' pain, find lowly balm for it!
   But now your trick has cost you, as tricks do:
   your guilt's my ransom, my guilt ransoms you.

CXXI

'Tis better to be vile than vile esteem'd,
When not to be receives reproach of being,
And the just pleasure lost which is so deem'd
Not by our feeling but by others' seeing:
For why should others' false adulterate eyes
Give salutation to my sportive blood?
Or on my frailties why are frailer spies,
Which in their wills count bad what I think good?
No, I am that I am, and they that level
At my abuses reckon up their own:
I may be straight, though they themselves be bevel;
By their rank thoughts my deeds must not be shown;
   Unless this general evil they maintain,
   All men are bad, and in their badness reign.

CXXII

Thy gift, thy tables, are within my brain
Full charactered with lasting memory,
Which shall above that idle rank remain
Beyond all date, even to eternity;
Or at the least, so long as brain and heart
Have faculty by nature to subsist;
Till each to razed oblivion yield his part
Of thee, thy record never can be miss'd.
That poor retention could not so much hold,
Nor need I tallies thy dear love to score;
Therefore to give them from me was I bold,
To trust those tables that receive thee more:
   To keep an adjunct to remember thee
   Were to import forgetfulness in me.

121 *Folk say I'm bad! All right, I'll...*

Bad-in-fact's good, but just-thought-bad is not.
A not-bad guy is put around as bad;
his lawful fun is lost to him: it's thought
bad, not by him, it's what folk saw and said.
For why should folks' unfair lascivious looks
insultingly accost my sporting blood?
I'm frail, but not as frail as spying spooks
who wilfully count bad what I think good.
No, I am that I am! A man who looks
at my faux pas must count up all his own:
mayhap I'm straight, and all such critics crooks,
wrong with rank thoughts to run my actions down:
    who might say, castigating all of us,
      mankind is bad, and bad is glorious.

122 *I didn't want your gift of a small blank book.*

Your gift, a jotting-book: all's in my brain,
no dross, full annotation, with facility
to last – no limit! – last and last again,
matching infinity's survivability.
Or, failing that: so long as brain ploughs on,
and spirit too shall naturally last
till both cut out in curt oblivion,
this your anthology stands firm and fast!
So much, that poor contraption could not hold;
I don't count up your loving with a tally.
That's why I put it out, I was that bold.
My brain absorbs you automatically:
    owning a gizmo for that happy grind
      would show I had a most oblivious mind.

CXXIII

No, Time, thou shalt not boast that I do change:
Thy pyramids built up with newer might
To me are nothing novel, nothing strange;
They are but dressings of a former sight.
Our dates are brief, and therefore we admire
What thou dost foist upon us that is old,
And rather make them born to our desire
Than think that we before have heard them told.
Thy registers and thee I both defy,
Not wondering at the present nor the past,
For thy records and what we see doth lie,
Made more or less by thy continual haste.
   This I do vow and this shall ever be;
   I will be true, despite thy scythe and thee.

CXXIV

If my dear love were but the child of state,
 It might for Fortune's bastard be unfather'd,
As subject to Time's love or to Time's hate,
Weeds among weeds, or flowers with flowers gather'd.
No, it was builded far from accident;
It suffers not in smiling pomp, nor falls
Under the blow of thralled discontent,
Whereto the inviting time our fashion calls:
It fears not policy, that heretic,
Which works on leases of short-number'd hours,
But all alone stands hugely politic,
That it nor grows with heat nor drowns with showers.
   To this I witness call the fools of time,
   Which die for goodness, who have lived for crime.

123 *Disdain for Chronology*

You hours, you shall not vaunt you that I vary!
You build your pyramids with instant might;
I call it unsurprising, ordinary,
just titivating a familiar sight.
Our span is short, which brings us to salaam
to what you foist upon us that is old,
counting it born according to our whim,
not thinking it a story known and told.
You and your data-stacks I hold in scorn,
admiring not days passing, nor days past:
you falsify your data, you suborn,
continually spurting, much too fast.
    This is my vow, which I'll not qualify:
      your scything won't curtail my constancy.

124 *Far surpassing political ups and downs,*
      swings of fashion...

My loving is not born of policy,
no bastard child of Luck without a dad,
not fashion's kiss nor animosity,
not in a bunch of jolly blooms, nor sad.
No, it was built far off from random quirk,
is not in thrall to smiling pomp, nor falls
victim to troublous blows impolitic,
to which our opportunist fashion calls:
it's not afraid of turncoat public mood,
which works by hiring a short count of hours,
but stands gigantic, solitary, good:
grows not with sunlight, drowns not with downpours.
    Mark this, I say, you fools historical,
      dying sanctimonious, though criminal!

CXXV

Were 't aught to me I bore the canopy,
With my extern the outward honouring,
Or laid great bases for eternity,
Which prove more short than waste or ruining?
Have I not seen dwellers on form and favour
Lose all, and more, by paying too much rent,
For compound sweet forgoing simple savour,
Pitiful thrivers, in their gazing spent?
No, let me be obsequious in thy heart,
And take thou my oblation, poor but free,
Which is not mix'd with seconds, knows no art,
But mutual render, only me for thee.
    Hence, thou suborn'd informer! a true soul
    When most impeach'd stands least in thy control.

CXXVI

O thou, my lovely boy, who in thy power
Dost hold Time's fickle glass, his sickle, hour;
Who hast by waning grown, and therein show'st
Thy lovers withering as thy sweet self grow'st;
If Nature, sovereign mistress over wrack,
As thou goest onwards, still will pluck thee back,
She keeps thee to this purpose, that her skill
May time disgrace and wretched minutes kill.
Yet fear her, O thou minion of her pleasure!
She may detain, but not still keep, her treasure:
    Her audit, though delay'd, answer'd must be,
    And her quietus is to render thee.

125 *Outward forms don't count. I worship you...*

What gain, did I hold up that canopy,
outwardly clutching, outwardly honouring?
Laid masonry for immortality
that won't outlast grim doom and ruining?
I saw inhabitants of form and favour
who lost it all, high outlay, low-point scraping,
gorging on compound sugars, not plain savour,
sumptuous, pitiful, worn out with gaping.
No, no: I worshipfully bow to you:
this my oblation's yours: it's just, though poor:
no taint of dross, it knows no art but mu-
-tual giving, just us two, that's what it's for.
   - Push off, paid spy! You tax a faithful soul
   with guilt: and that is not in your control.

126 *Natura can hold Anno Domini at bay*
for only so long.

My chuck, with Tick-Tock's hourglass in your hand,
you thwart his pruning-hook: your looks withstand
waning of light, you flourish, and you show
your darlings wilting, as you grandly grow.
Watch how Natura, royal boss of wrack,
still from your dissolution plucks you back:
Natura guards you, purposing to kill
Sir Tick-Tock's noxious hours with shaming skill.
Ah, but look out, Natura's toyboy minion!
Natura flaunts, but can't prolong, dominion.
Await that audit, it's not optional,
you'll sign your quitting, you shall pay in full.

You may push out Natura with a pitchfork –
but Natura's coming right back at you!
So says Roman bard Quintus Horatius Flaccus.

CXXVII

In the old age black was not counted fair,
Or if it were, it bore not beauty's name;
But now is black beauty's successive heir,
And beauty slander'd with a bastard shame:
For since each hand hath put on nature's power,
Fairing the foul with art's false borrow'd face,
Sweet beauty hath no name, no holy bower,
But is profaned, if not lives in disgrace.
Therefore my mistress' brows are raven black,
Her eyes so suited, and they mourners seem
At such who, not born fair, no beauty lack,
Slandering creation with a false esteem:
    Yet so they mourn, becoming of their woe,
    That every tongue says beauty should look so.

CXXVIII

How oft, when thou, my music, music play'st,
Upon that blessed wood whose motion sounds
With thy sweet fingers, when thou gently sway'st
The wiry concord that mine ear confounds,
Do I envy those jacks that nimble leap
To kiss the tender inward of thy hand,
Whilst my poor lips, which should that harvest reap,
At the wood's boldness by thee blushing stand!
To be so tickled, they would change their state
And situation with those dancing chips,
O'er whom thy fingers walk with gentle gait,
Making dead wood more blest than living lips.
    Since saucy jacks so happy are in this,
    Give them thy fingers, me thy lips to kiss.

127 Black's OK, Warpaint isn't: my Lady is Dark

Long, long ago, black didn't count as bonny,
or if it did, hung out no boastful bush:
but now black's got good-looking's patrimony,
good looks cop calumny, with bastard's blush.
Now all our hands usurp all natural laws,
fairing what's foul with art's mascara'd brow:
fair form is just thrown out, anonymous,
not holy, anyway not glorious, now.
That's why my lady's orbs of sight, as black
as garb of mourning, must purport to mourn
at folk, fair not by birth but by no lack
of art, who put God's handiwork to scorn.
　　This dismal mourning suits my lady, though:
　　so much, that all say good looks should look so.

128 You play that lucky virginal. Play my lips!

What lucky wood, if you, my music, play
virginal music! For its motion sounds
with your carousing digits, as you sway
its wiry concord that my soul confounds:
and I'm invidious! Quays that nimbly spring
to kiss your soft and lissom inward hand,
whilst my poor lips miss out on haymaking,
blush at wood's hardihood, and idly stand!
To win my mouth such tingling, I would swap
its situation with yon dancing chips,
on which your digits walk with touch tip-top,
prioritising wood, not living lips.
　　It's bliss for saucy quays, to kiss (grant this!)
　　your digits. Grant my wish, your lips to kiss!

Quays (sic*): parts of virginals or of a harpsichord,
possibly clad with ivory, forming a quayboard:
apt for rapid touch of your hands.*

CXXIX

The expense of spirit in a waste of shame
Is lust in action; and till action, lust
Is perjured, murderous, bloody, full of blame,
Savage, extreme, rude, cruel, not to trust,
Enjoy'd no sooner but despised straight,
Past reason hunted, and no sooner had,
Past reason hated, as a swallow'd bait
On purpose laid to make the taker mad;
Mad in pursuit and in possession so;
Had, having, and in quest to have, extreme;
A bliss in proof, and proved, a very woe;
Before, a joy proposed; behind, a dream.
   All this the world well knows; yet none knows well
   To shun the heaven that leads men to this hell.

CXXX

My mistress' eyes are nothing like the sun;
Coral is far more red than her lips' red;
If snow be white, why then her breasts are dun;
If hairs be wires, black wires grow on her head.
I have seen roses damask'd, red and white,
But no such roses see I in her cheeks;
And in some perfumes is there more delight
Than in the breath that from my mistress reeks.
I love to hear her speak, yet well I know
That music hath a far more pleasing sound;
I grant I never saw a goddess go;
My mistress, when she walks, treads on the ground:
   And yet, by heaven, I think my love as rare
   As any she belied with false compare.

129 *Disgusting Outlay of Spirit*

In shaming swamp our vital spirit spilling
is lust in action; and, till action, lust
is bloody, traitorous and sinful killing,
manic, uncouth, atrocious, not to trust;
a quick-fix joy that turns to loathing, straight;
a crazy craving; soon as it is had,
irrationally odious; a bait
laid for you, which has caught you, struck you mad;
mad in pursuit, in acquisition too;
had, having, hunting, all incongruous;
bliss with no proof, proving no bliss to you;
looks fun at first, in hindsight fatuous.
    So much is known; but who can tutor us?
    How to cut out this trip to Tartarus?

130 *A Gallant Comparison*

My lady's orbs can't match two Suns at noon;
coral, too ruddy, trumps my lady's lip;
snow shows my lady's bosom slushy-brown;
black wiry hairs top out my ladyship;
carnations, snow or crimson, don't abound
around my lady's physiognomy;
as for aromas, it was always found,
my lady's just unsatisfactory;
though to my lady's larynx I'm in thrall,
it falls a long way short of musical;
gods of Olympus probably walk tall;
my lady's gait's not astro-magical.
    Don't worry, though: my girl can still surpass
    Any too crassly sold and broadcast lass.

CXXXI

Thou art as tyrannous, so as thou art,
As those whose beauties proudly make them cruel;
For well thou know'st to my dear doting heart
Thou art the fairest and most precious jewel.
Yet, in good faith, some say that thee behold
Thy face hath not the power to make love groan:
To say they err I dare not be so bold,
Although I swear it to myself alone.
And, to be sure that is not false I swear,
A thousand groans, but thinking on thy face,
One on another's neck, do witness bear
Thy black is fairest in my judgment's place.
   In nothing art thou black save in thy deeds,
   And thence this slander, as I think, proceeds.

CXXXII

Thine eyes I love, and they, as pitying me,
Knowing thy heart torments me with disdain,
Have put on black and loving mourners be,
Looking with pretty ruth upon my pain.
And truly not the morning sun of heaven
Better becomes the grey cheeks of the east,
Nor that full star that ushers in the even
Doth half that glory to the sober west,
As those two mourning eyes become thy face:
O, let it then as well beseem thy heart
To mourn for me, since mourning doth thee grace,
And suit thy pity like in every part.
   Then will I swear beauty herself is black
   And all they foul that thy complexion lack.

131 *Thou art Tyrannous, but Stunning*

Thou art as tyrannous, so as thou art,
as any who look good and turn out vicious.
You know your status in my inmost part:
a diamond brooch, top dollar, bootylicious.
many say frankly, looking at you cold,
'This isn't stunning. Would a suitor groan?'
But I say – not out loud, I'm not so bold –
I say 'What liars!' if I'm on my own.
I say it on my oath – I truly know
my thousand groans about your physiognomy
(my phiz has lain with yours!) all go to show
your dark is shiny-bright, in my taxonomy.
    You look top-class. It's only what you do:
    That's why so many folk complain of you.

132 *So gloriously dark, you mourn my pain!*

Your darling optic orbs pity my plight,
knowing you rack my body with disdain,
loving and mourning too, clad black as night,
and most alluring, gazing on my pain.
And truly, matutinal sun's no match
for you in gracing dawn's primordial gray,
nor's that big moon that twilight puts on watch,
which adds its glory to a dying day.
Not sun, not moon, but your two orbs that mourn
adorn you most: with luck your mainspring too
will mourn my plight, for mourning can adorn
you, looking good in any part of you.
    I'll say on oath that fair is truly black;
    and foul, all who your coloration lack.

CXXXIII

Beshrew that heart that makes my heart to groan
For that deep wound it gives my friend and me!
Is't not enough to torture me alone,
But slave to slavery my sweet'st friend must be?
Me from myself thy cruel eye hath taken,
And my next self thou harder hast engross'd:
Of him, myself, and thee, I am forsaken;
A torment thrice threefold thus to be cross'd.
Prison my heart in thy steel bosom's ward,
But then my friend's heart let my poor heart bail;
Whoe'er keeps me, let my heart be his guard;
Thou canst not then use rigour in my gaol:
   And yet thou wilt; for I, being pent in thee,
   Perforce am thine, and all that is in me.

CXXXIV

So, now I have confess'd that he is thine,
And I myself am mortgaged to thy will,
Myself I'll forfeit, so that other mine
Thou wilt restore, to be my comfort still:
But thou wilt not, nor he will not be free,
For thou art covetous and he is kind;
He learn'd but surety-like to write for me
Under that bond that him as fast doth bind.
The statute of thy beauty thou wilt take,
Thou usurer, that put'st forth all to use,
And sue a friend came debtor for my sake;
So him I lose through my unkind abuse.
   Him have I lost; thou hast both him and me:
   He pays the whole, and yet am I not free.

133 *That Woman's Mixing it with my Buddy*

Down with that soul that puts my soul in pain
for that bad wound it brings my bro and I !
My buddy's wrapt in chain on slavish chain:
can't I sip, on my own, this agony?
I'm split by your harsh orb, I'm split in two;
my buddy's lot was hard, and you could swallow.
I am forsook by him and I and you,
crossing a triply trinal pain and sorrow.
Prison my soul in your iron bosom's ward,
and my poor soul can pay my buddy's bail.
My jailbird soul my buddy's soul shall guard,
so you won't show much rigour in my jail!
    Show it you will, though; for I'm caught in you,
    yours by constraint, and all my all is too.

134 *Woman! You got him, you got your way.*
And I'm...

So, as I said just now, you got my bro,
and I'm in hock to you and to your will.
I'll pay, I'll swap you my poor body, so
you'll manumit my bro, my comfort still.
But you won't do it, won't unlatch my chuck:
you grasp and grip and clutch! My chuck is kind,
but, signing as my guarantor, got stuck,
caught by that bond that has him in a bind.
Using your looks, you put your full amount,
as is your lawful right, on usury,
racking my buddy, skint on my account.
I lost him, thanks to your malignity.
    I lost him, and you got him, and yours truly;
    my pal's paid all; I'm still in clink, unduly.

*Manumit: in antiquity, to acquit a bondsman
or bondswoman from that unhappy civil status.*

CXXXV

Whoever hath her wish, thou hast thy 'Will,'
And 'Will' to boot, and 'Will' in overplus;
More than enough am I that vex thee still,
To thy sweet will making addition thus.
Wilt thou, whose will is large and spacious,
Not once vouchsafe to hide my will in thine?
Shall will in others seem right gracious,
And in my will no fair acceptance shine?
The sea all water, yet receives rain still
And in abundance addeth to his store;
So thou, being rich in 'Will', add to thy 'Will'
One will of mine, to make thy large 'Will' more.
   Let no unkind, no fair beseechers kill;
   Think all but one, and me in that one 'Will.'

CXXXVI

If thy soul check thee that I come so near,
Swear to thy blind soul that I was thy 'Will,'
And will, thy soul knows, is admitted there;
Thus far for love my love-suit, sweet, fulfil.
'Will' will fulfil the treasure of thy love,
Ay, fill it full with wills, and my will one.
In things of great receipt with ease we prove
Among a number one is reckon'd none:
Then in the number let me pass untold,
Though in thy stores' account I one must be;
For nothing hold me, so it please thee hold
That nothing me, a something sweet to thee:
   Make but my name thy love, and love that still,
   And then thou lovest me, for my name is 'Will.'

135 *Won't you just plump for 'Will'?*

If many had a wish, thou hast thy 'Will',
And 'Will' to boot, and 'Will' to boot plus plus;
I'm all abundant to accost you still,
on your will, laying an addition, thus.
Won't you – you know your will is big and spacious –
kindly vouchsafing, clasp my will in yours?
Shall a third party's will turn out right gracious,
And my will fail to pass your shining doors?
Th' Atlantic's fully liquid, but rain still
Falls copiously in and bulks its mass:
Can't you, so rich in 'Will', add to your 'Will'
Just this my will, and so your 'Will' surpass?
　　And no unkindly No should suitors kill:
　　Think wills, click unity: think I'm that 'Will'.

136 *I'm your Will who will Fulfil...*

If your soul jibs at my introitus,
say to your blind soul that I was your Will,
and will, your soul knows, has a right to pass;
so, loving lass, my loving-suit fulfil.
Will will fulfil your Cupid's-box of magic,
so fill it full with wills, and count my will!
In things of quantity it's axiomatic
that singularity will count as nil:
so in that vast crowd I shall pass untold,
though in your shop's account I am a thing;
hold it as nothing, only kindly hold
that nothing, which I am, as your darling.
　　Swoon for my monica, go swooning still:
　　swoon for yours truly, who am known as 'Will'.

CXXXVII

Thou blind fool, Love, what dost thou to mine eyes,
That they behold, and see not what they see?
They know what beauty is, see where it lies,
Yet what the best is take the worst to be.
If eyes corrupt by over-partial looks
Be anchor'd in the bay where all men ride,
Why of eyes' falsehood hast thou forged hooks,
Whereto the judgment of my heart is tied?
Why should my heart think that a several plot
Which my heart knows the wide world's common place?
Or mine eyes seeing this, say this is not,
To put fair truth upon so foul a face?
   In things right true my heart and eyes have erred,
   And to this false plague are they now transferr'd.

CXXXVIII

When my love swears that she is made of truth
I do believe her, though I know she lies,
That she might think me some untutor'd youth,
Unlearned in the world's false subtleties.
Thus vainly thinking that she thinks me young,
Although she knows my days are past the best,
Simply I credit her false speaking tongue:
On both sides thus is simple truth suppress'd.
But wherefore says she not she is unjust?
And wherefore say not I that I am old?
O, love's best habit is in seeming trust,
And age in love loves not to have years told:
   Therefore I lie with her and she with me,
   And in our faults by lies we flatter'd be.

137 *My sight and my gut instinct both got it badly wrong.*

Cupid, blind fool, what dost thou to my sight?
I look at - that! - but look! my looking's off.
I know its looks, I know its lair all right,
but in my sight, bad stuff is just good stuff.
If sight, corrupt by all-too-partial looks,
drops anchor in that bay of busy riding,
why of sight's fictions hast thou wrought sharp hooks
to snag my gut's thoughts with injurious guiding?
Why should my gut think it's a just-yours plot,
knowing it's vulgar ground of common count?
Why should my sight sight this and say it's not,
to put fair truth upon so foul a front?
    My sight and gut both got it wrong, and so
    in fallacy and plaguy blight must go.

138 *Truth about Youth? Lying with my Lady.*

My lady says on oath 'I'm built of truth!'
I swallow it, but know my lady's lying,
and thinks no doubt I am a callow youth
all ignorant of worldly falsifying.
Thus vainly thinking 'Madam thinks I'm young,'
though madam knows my glory-day is past,
I trust what that two-timing throat has sung,
and so by both of us plain truth is lost.
But can't my lady say 'I am unjust'?
And why don't I admit that I am old?
O! Loving's good in garb of outward trust,
and loving dotards don't want birthdays told.
    I'm lying with my liar lying by,
    both, in our faults, lying obligingly.

CXXXIX

O, call not me to justify the wrong
That thy unkindness lays upon my heart;
Wound me not with thine eye but with thy tongue;
Use power with power and slay me not by art.
Tell me thou lovest elsewhere, but in my sight,
Dear heart, forbear to glance thine eye aside:
What nee"st thou wound with cunning when thy might
Is more than my o'er-press'd defence can bide?
Let me excuse thee: ah! my love well knows
Her pretty looks have been mine enemies,
And therefore from my face she turns my foes,
That they elsewhere might dart their injuries:
    Yet do not so; but since I am near slain,
    Kill me outright with looks and rid my pain.

CXL

Be wise as thou art cruel; do not press
My tongue-tied patience with too much disdain;
Lest sorrow lend me words and words express
The manner of my pity-wanting pain.
If I might teach thee wit, better it were,
Though not to love, yet, love, to tell me so;
As testy sick men, when their deaths be near,
No news but health from their physicians know;
For if I should despair, I should grow mad,
And in my madness might speak ill of thee:
Now this ill-wresting world is grown so bad,
Mad slanderers by mad ears believed be,
    That I may not be so, nor thou belied,
    Bear thine eyes straight, though thy proud heart go wide.

139 *So Good-Looking that it Hurts*

Don't think that I shall justify this hurt
that you inflict, unkind, on my soft part;
don't do it with a look, but with a word:
apply strong hands to slay, not skilful art;
say X or Y's your crush: but in my sight
kindly don't turn away to snatch a look.
Why would you wound with cunning, you who might
go for a knockout with your big right hook?
I'll put this gloss on it: my darling knows
such stunning looks can function to my cost:
and so my woman turns away, and shows
that pair of gun-ports to a random host.
    Don't do it, though: you know I'm almost slain:
    a look will kill outright, and rid my pain.

140 *Say kind things so that I don't go crazy.*

Add wisdom to your sadism: don't crush
my stoic stumbling with too much disdain;
sorrow might run to words, and out might rush
strong hints about my pity-wanting pain.
If I might just instruct you, right? You might
maintain, although not loving, that you do:
gruff invalids approaching 'that good night'
obtain no word but 'Right as rain, that's you'.
If I'm struck *hoffnungslos*, I should go mad,
might madly smirch that dignity of yours;
now that this twisting world has grown so bad,
mad castigators find mad auditors.
    No dirt on you! I mustn't go that way!
    Look straight, although your inmost part may stray.

Hoffnungslos: having nothing at all in Pandora's box.

CXLI

In faith, I do not love thee with mine eyes,
For they in thee a thousand errors note;
But 'tis my heart that loves what they despise,
Who in despite of view is pleased to dote;
Nor are mine ears with thy tongue's tune delighted,
Nor tender feeling, to base touches prone,
Nor taste, nor smell, desire to be invited
To any sensual feast with thee alone:
But my five wits nor my five senses can
Dissuade one foolish heart from serving thee,
Who leaves unsway'd the likeness of a man,
Thy proud heart's slave and vassal wretch to be:
    Only this far I count my blight my gain,
    That she that makes me sin awards me pain.

CXLII

Love is my sin and thy dear virtue hate,
Hate of my sin, grounded on sinful loving:
O, but with mine compare thou thine own state,
And thou shalt find it merits not reproving;
Or, if it do, not from those lips of thine,
That have profaned their scarlet ornaments
And seal'd false bonds of love as oft as mine,
Robb'd others' beds' revenues of their rents.
Be it lawful I love thee, as thou lovest those
Whom thine eyes woo as mine importune thee:
Root pity in thy heart, that when it grows
Thy pity may deserve to pitied be.
    If thou dost seek to have what thou dost hide,
    By self-example mayst thou be denied!

141 Against all visual &c. data, I'm stuck on you.

It's not my sight that worships you. My oath!
A thousand faults in you assault my sight.
No, my gut worships you, though sight is loth:
ignoring sight, it's fond of you, all right.
My auditory whorls don't dig your song;
my touch-pads, aiming low, don't fancy you,
nor lip, nor nostril: so don't ask along
this gang to join your solitary do.
My clutch of wits, my clutch of inputs can
not sway my foolish gut from following
you, who dismasts what's not in fact a man,
in thrall to your proud soul, a slavish thing.
    Only my blight thus far I count my gain:
    you prompt my sin and you inflict my pain.

142 You and I and Our Sins (Yours, Mostly)

Loving's my sin; your shining skill is loathing:
loathing my sin, you build on sinful loving.
But in comparison with yours, it's nothing –
my sin is small, no call for gruff improving;
or anyway, not from such lips as yours!
Shaming that sumptuous crimson with your sin,
slyly mis-bonding (and my sin concurs),
you harm cashflows of crashpads that cash in.
You must allow my loving you, although
you go round ogling: not my faithful fashion.
Root pity in your soul, and it will grow:
Your pity may, at last, incur compassion.
    You aim at having that which you withhold:
    Fair's fair, you know! With luck, your luck won't hold.

CXLIII

Lo! as a careful housewife runs to catch
One of her feather'd creatures broke away,
Sets down her babe and makes all swift dispatch
In pursuit of the thing she would have stay,
Whilst her neglected child holds her in chase,
Cries to catch her whose busy care is bent
To follow that which flies before her face,
Not prizing her poor infant's discontent;
So runn'st thou after that which flies from thee,
Whilst I thy babe chase thee afar behind;
But if thou catch thy hope, turn back to me,
And play the mother's part, kiss me, be kind:
   So will I pray that thou mayst have thy 'Will',
   If thou turn back, and my loud crying still.

CXLIV

Two loves I have of comfort and despair,
Which like two spirits do suggest me still:
The better angel is a man right fair,
The worser spirit a woman colour'd ill.
To win me soon to hell, my female evil
Tempteth my better angel from my side,
And would corrupt my saint to be a devil,
Wooing his purity with her foul pride.
And whether that my angel be turn'd fiend
Suspect I may, but not directly tell;
But being both from me, both to each friend,
I guess one angel in another's hell:
   Yet this shall I ne'er know, but live in doubt,
   Till my bad angel fire my good one out.

143 Backyard Drama: Chasing your Barnstorming Bantam

Look, as a thrifty woman runs to catch
poultry, a bantam-cock that got away,
puts baby down and with all swift dispatch
pursuing, hunts that bird that ought to stay;
abandoning a baby which in turn
follows on, crying to a mum too busy
trying to catch a bantam, and who'll spurn
turning to stop this yowling infant's tizzy;
that's how you run, towards what scrams from you,
whilst I, your baby, run in far pursuit;
but if you catch your wish, turn backward, do,
and play a momma's part, and kindly put
    a kiss! I'll pray you gain your way and Will,
      if you turn back, my loud complaint to still.

144 Good spirit, bad spirit: my two darlings. Or not.

My two amours: this, comfort; that, sharp pain:
two spirit-birds assailing, haunting still.
Good spirit is a good, good-looking man;
bad spirit, murky lass, a shady jill.
To quickly damn my soul, my woman shook
my good man up, to win him from my arms,
and would corrupt my saint into a spook,
wooing his purity with filthy charms.
Is my good spirit naughty now? I may
harbour suspicion, but I cannot suss.
Both pals in club-of-two, and both away!
I fancy good is in bad's Tartarus.
    But I'm not going to know: I'm caught in doubt,
      till my bad woman blasts my good man out.

CXLV

Those lips that Love's own hand did make
Breathed forth the sound that said 'I hate'
To me that languish'd for her sake;
But when she saw my woeful state,
Straight in her heart did mercy come,
Chiding that tongue that ever sweet
Was used in giving gentle doom,
And taught it thus anew to greet:
'I hate' she alter'd with an end,
That follow'd it as gentle day
Doth follow night, who like a fiend
From heaven to hell is flown away;
　'I hate' from hate away she threw,
　And saved my life, saying 'not you.'

CXLVI

Poor soul, the centre of my sinful earth,
[　] these rebel powers that thee array;
Why dost thou pine within and suffer dearth,
Painting thy outward walls so costly gay?
Why so large cost, having so short a lease,
Dost thou upon thy fading mansion spend?
Shall worms, inheritors of this excess,
Eat up thy charge? is this thy body's end?
Then soul, live thou upon thy servant's loss,
And let that pine to aggravate thy store;
Buy terms divine in selling hours of dross;
Within be fed, without be rich no more:
　So shalt thou feed on Death, that feeds on men,
　And Death once dead, there's no more dying then.

145 *My lady isn't talking about hating now.*

That mouth that's wrought by Cupid's hand
put out a sound of *'I abhor'*
as I lay faint and could not stand;
but spotting I was in a poor
way, straightaway took pity and,
chiding that organ unctuous
that smoothly said things ominous,
taught it a trick for talking right,
putting on *'I abhor'* a tail
that follows it as day doth night,
(that diabolic imp, in flight
from Halls of Bliss, down Gloomy Trail):
   and hath away *'I'm hating'* cast,
    (my saviour!) with *'not you'* at last.

Possibly matrimonial, about Ms Hathaway.

146 *Nourish your inward soul,*
     not your outward body.

Poor soul, you midpoint of my sinful soil,
facing puissant hostility's array,
why languish inwardly with haggard toil,
painting your outward walls so costly gay?
So vast a cost, so short an occupation:
why pour it on a mansion bound to vanish?
Shall worms, to whom shall pass your dissipation,
gulp it all down? Is this your body's finish?
Soul, draw down vigour from your minion's loss:
its languishing shall grow your almonry.
Buy godly funds, unloading hours of dross.
Inward nutrition! Outward scarcity!
   Sup on Mortality, that sups on all:
    hit Dying with his final dying fall.

CXLVII

My love is as a fever, longing still
For that which longer nurseth the disease,
Feeding on that which doth preserve the ill,
The uncertain sickly appetite to please.
My reason, the physician to my love,
Angry that his prescriptions are not kept,
Hath left me, and I desperate now approve
Desire is death, which physic did except.
Past cure I am, now reason is past care,
And frantic-mad with evermore unrest;
My thoughts and my discourse as madmen's are,
At random from the truth vainly express'd;
    For I have sworn thee fair and thought thee bright,
    Who art as black as hell, as dark as night.

CXLVIII

O me, what eyes hath Love put in my head,
Which have no correspondence with true sight!
Or, if they have, where is my judgment fled,
That censures falsely what they see aright?
If that be fair whereon my false eyes dote,
What means the world to say it is not so?
If it be not, then love doth well denote
Love's eye is not so true as all men's 'No.'
How can it? O, how can Love's eye be true,
That is so vex'd with watching and with tears?
No marvel then, though I mistake my view;
The sun itself sees not till heaven clears.
    O cunning Love! with tears thou keep'st me blind,
    Lest eyes well-seeing thy foul faults should find.

147 I'm incurably sick with loving you, you nasty bit of work.

My passion's as a quinsy, longing still
for that which but prolongs my malady,
lapping up anything that works my ill,
a lulling, gulling, toxic pharmacy.
My mind, my doctor in this passion's thrall,
angry that I don't act as I am bid,
has slung its hook; not hoping now, I call
my crush my doom, for all that physick did.
My mind's past caring, I'm past curing too,
and frantic-mad with lasting disarray:
all that I think and say is loopy-loo,
in vain, and random. Truth is far away!
   I'd sworn your soul was fair, I thought it bright:
   thou'rt black as Tartarus, and dark as night.

148 Ophthalmic Drawbacks with Cupid

O my, what pupils lurk amid my brows,
put in by Cupid, void of rightful sight!
Or - if it's rightful - what distorts my nous
to wrongful judging, though my sight is right?
If 'x' looks good, as my bad orbs portray:
now, why should folk proclaim it is not so?
If it's not so, my loving sight's astray,
simply not up to common scratch! Ah, no,
How can it, how can loving sight work rightly,
that is so fraught with watching, damp with crying?
It's unsurprising that my sight's unsightly:
isn't bright sunlight blind, till clouds go flying?
   Smart Cupid squirts my pupils, and I'm blind
   to his foul faults, which, with dry orbs, I'd find.

CXLIX

Canst thou, O cruel! say I love thee not,
When I against myself with thee partake?
Do I not think on thee, when I forgot
Am of myself, all tyrant, for thy sake?
Who hateth thee that I do call my friend?
On whom frown'st thou that I do fawn upon?
Nay, if thou lour'st on me, do I not spend
Revenge upon myself with present moan?
What merit do I in myself respect,
That is so proud thy service to despise,
When all my best doth worship thy defect,
Commanded by the motion of thine eyes?
   But, love, hate on, for now I know thy mind;
   Those that can see thou lovest, and I am blind.

CL

O, from what power hast thou this powerful might
With insufficiency my heart to sway?
To make me give the lie to my true sight,
And swear that brightness doth not grace the day?
Whence hast thou this becoming of things ill,
That in the very refuse of thy deeds
There is such strength and warrantize of skill
That, in my mind, thy worst all best exceeds?
Who taught thee how to make me love thee more
The more I hear and see just cause of hate?
O, though I love what others do abhor,
With others thou shouldst not abhor my state:
   If thy unworthiness raised love in me,
   More worthy I to be beloved of thee.

149 *Obviously I long for you, although you...*

Tyrant, I long for you! You can't say not:
siding with you, I'm doing down yours truly.
I think about you always, I forgot
my honour, and it profits you unduly.
Nobody hating you may grasp my hand;
I fawn on nobody that you disdain;
no, if you frown, it's tit for tat! I stand
as my own castigator, trading pain.
Can I find any worth in my poor soul,
that proudly ought to spurn your witching thrall?
to my good part, your faults look worshipful:
slavish to your twin orbs' sign manual.
   Go right on hating, chuck: I know your mind:
    it's sight that fans your fancy, and I'm blind.

150 *O! How do I put up with this?*

What god has laid on you this puissant might?
You fall so short, and I fall in your sway!
And I discard plain signals of my sight,
insist that no bright light adorns a day.
How do you look so good by boding ill?
Far down that rubbish-bin of all you do,
you pack a punch, a warranty of skill:
and all that's good can't match what's worst in you.
Who taught you how to rack my passion tight
with loathly sights and sounds I'd shrink from, justly?
I long for that which puts all folks to flight.
Don't spurn my crisis: all folks do: it's ghastly!
   Your falling short is what kick-starts my loving:
    which ought to start you mutually moving.

CLI

Love is too young to know what conscience is;
Yet who knows not conscience is born of love?
Then, gentle cheater, urge not my amiss,
Lest guilty of my faults thy sweet self prove:
For, thou betraying me, I do betray
My nobler part to my gross body's treason;
My soul doth tell my body that he may
Triumph in love; flesh stays no farther reason;
But, rising at thy name, doth point out thee
As his triumphant prize. Proud of this pride,
He is contented thy poor drudge to be,
To stand in thy affairs, fall by thy side.
 No want of conscience hold it that I call
 Her 'love' for whose dear love I rise and fall.

CLII

In loving thee thou know'st I am forsworn,
But thou art twice forsworn, to me love swearing,
In act thy bed-vow broke and new faith torn,
In vowing new hate after new love bearing.
But why of two oaths' breach do I accuse thee,
When I break twenty? I am perjured most;
For all my vows are oaths but to misuse thee
And all my honest faith in thee is lost,
For I have sworn deep oaths of thy deep kindness,
Oaths of thy love, thy truth, thy constancy,
And, to enlighten thee, gave eyes to blindness,
Or made them swear against the thing they see;
 For I have sworn thee fair; more perjured I,
 To swear against the truth so foul a lie!

151 *Faults, Guilt, Body & Soul: a lot of Cunning Punning!*

Cupid's too young, cannot know right from wrong:
but isn't that what loving can contrast?
So, kindly traitor, sing no grudging song
about my faults: your guilt may blush, at last.
If you play traitor, I play traitor too,
my soul is sold to my gross body's sin;
my soul winds up my body: Go on, you
may triumph! – Body's quickly wading in,
and rising, points at you triumphantly,
his spoils of war, so proud and glorious,
happy to toil as your poor dogsbody,
stand in your doings, fall contiguous!
    Don't think I'm nonchalant, if I should call
    'darling', that nymph for whom I mount and fall.

152 *Thou'rt Doubly Forsworn: I Surpass That by a Long Way.*

In loving you, you know I am forsworn,
But doubly thou'rt forsworn: for first thou swor'st
loving, but brok'st thy vow; and thy faith's torn,
now vowing loathing, thou who loving bor'st.
But why do I indict you, doubly vicious?
Two oaths? But I can add a nought! I'm most
forsworn, for I vow only what's fictitious,
traducing you: through you my faith's all lost.
Many an oath I took that thou art kind,
oaths of thy loving, truth and constancy;
to light you up, I struck my pupils blind
with oaths against all visibility.
    My oath: you, fair, not foul! Forsworn am I:
    against all truth, so foul a falsity!

CLIII

Cupid laid by his brand, and fell asleep:
A maid of Dian's this advantage found,
And his love-kindling fire did quickly steep
In a cold valley-fountain of that ground;
Which borrow'd from this holy fire of Love
A dateless lively heat, still to endure,
And grew a seething bath, which yet men prove
Against strange maladies a sovereign cure.
But at my mistress' eye Love's brand new-fired,
The boy for trial needs would touch my breast;
I, sick withal, the help of bath desired,
And thither hied, a sad distemper'd guest,
    But found no cure: the bath for my help lies
    Where Cupid got new fire--my mistress' eyes.

CLIV

The little Love-god lying once asleep
Laid by his side his heart-inflaming brand,
Whilst many nymphs that vow'd chaste life to keep
Came tripping by; but in her maiden hand
The fairest votary took up that fire
Which many legions of true hearts had warm'd;
And so the general of hot desire
Was sleeping by a virgin hand disarm'd.
This brand she quenched in a cool well by,
Which from Love's fire took heat perpetual,
Growing a bath and healthful remedy
For men diseased; but I, my mistress' thrall,
    Came there for cure, and this by that I prove,
    Love's fire heats water, water cools not love.

153 Cupid's Torch was put in a Pond;
my Lady's Twin Orbs

Cupid, just nodding off, put down his brand.
Diana's maid got lucky: having found
his passion-kindling torch, trod smartly and
dipt it in a cold pond that lay around.
Acquiring from that amorous holy torch
a high tog rating and a warmth undying,
it's now a good hot bath (though wouldn't scorch)
for odd conditions: doctors go on trying.
Ah! but my lady's orb was bright, and lit it;
Cupid must try it, touch it to my trunk;
so I was poorly, thought 'Bath Road!' and hit it,
a sad sick invalid, in sorrow sunk.
    No good! A salving bath my lady's got:
    twin orbs: and Cupid's torch was burning hot!

154 Cupid's Glym in a Fountain,
& My Lady's Glamour

Cupid, young god, was drowsing fitfully
and laid apart his passion-kindling brand,
whilst many nymphs with vows of chastity
swung past his cot. At last with virgin hand
a most fair votary took up that glym
by which so many darlings had grown warm,
intacta manu lifting it from him,
hot passion's Admiral, and did disarm,
dousing his brand in a cool fountain by,
which took undying warmth from Cupid's link,
making a bath to staunch a malady
of sorry invalids: but I don't think
    it works. Poor thrall I, to my lady's glamour:
    Amor may warm a bath; no bath cools Amor.

~

THAT'S ALL,
FOLKS!

~

Three cheers! these revels ended:
Verse Perec never penned.
We teetered, slewed, descended:
We persevered. The End.

Index of Will's Sonnets' First Lines

~

Other publications by Timothy Adès
rhyming translator-poet, mostly from French:

33 Sonnets of the Resistance and other poems, by Jean Cassou. Arc Publications, 2002, 2005. Bilingual text

How to be a Grandfather, by Victor Hugo, 2002, Complete Edition 2012. Hearing Eye. English text

The Madness of Amadis and other poems, by Jean Cassou. Agenda Editions, 2008. Bilingual text

The Big Story of the Lion by Victor Hugo, 2013. Hearing Eye. Fold-out, pictures, English text

Florentino and the Devil, by Alberto Arvelo Torrealba. Shearsman Books, 2014. Spanish. Bilingual text

Storysongs/Chantefables, by Robert Desnos, Agenda Editions, 2014. Pictures, bilingual text.

Robert Desnos, Surrealist, Lover, Resistant. Arc Publications, 2016. Bilingual text.

www.timothyades.com

Other publications by Dempsey & Windle

A Barrel of Monkeys (ed Janice Windle) 978-1-907435-28-7

The Cul-de-Sac Less Travelled Ray Diamond 978-1-907435-34-8

Being Dragged Across the Carpet by the Cat Dónall Dempsey 978-1-907435-23-2

The Equator and Other Disappointments Trisha Broomfield 978-1-907135-33-1

Thor's Light Richard Sellwood 978-1-907435-32-4

The Smell of Purple Dónall Dempsey 978-1-907435-19-5

The Keystone Anthology (ed Janice Windle) 978-1-907435-30-0

Loving the Light Janice Windle 978-1-907435-14-0

How to Make a Dress Out of Silence Janice Windle 978-1-907435-13-3

www.dempseyandwindle.co.uk

About Lipograms

Lipograms go back to antiquity. A man from Aranda had his way with your blind bard's *Iliad* - fall of Troy and all that - writing its first book without an alpha, and so on, going straight through. Tryphiodorus did as much for that strong and crafty man on his way to Ithaca, who slid past Scylla and Charybdis, spikily fooling a Cyclops and slothfully frolicking with Calypso, and finally caught up with his son and his missus again. Mr. Isaac D-- had a similar habit - his son was Victoria's most flamboyant politician. *La Disparition* is a whodunit by a Parisian with big hair and a cat, skilfully brought to us from Calais by a translator as *A Void*. *Oulipo* is a group of lipogrammatists: this curious word is short for *'Workshop of Writing Possibility'*. *Lipo-* is from Plato's word for *omit* (not his similar word for *fat*, as in liposuction). I could go on...

~

Timothy A is an award-winning rhyming translator of Victor Hugo's last lyrical book, focusing on his young family... also of Hugo's gallant and scholarly compatriot Cassou, who found inspiration in a Vichy prison and in poor distrait Amadis of Gaul: two bilingual books of Cassou. Add a fold-out, a Big Story about a Lion: this too is by Hugo. Timothy's fourth book is *Storysongs*, thirty animal talismans with brilliant illustrations by Cat Zaza; a fifth is forthcoming from Arc Publications, again by *Storysongs'* witty and wondrous author, son of a Paris poultryman, who broadcast his *Ballad of Fantomas* as a radio play, found bliss with Youki Foujita, fought against Nazism, and was its victim; and a sixth, from Spanish, is a dramatic singing and rapid-rhyming all-night showdown among ranch-hands on a vast plain in Barinas, inland from Caracas: a human champion of his art, confronting Satan, risking all!

This is Timothy's first book in Inglish.